PAGES FROM
A MUSICIAN'S LIFE

Pages from a Musician's Life

FRITZ BUSCH

Translated by
MARJORIE STRACHEY

GREENWOOD PRESS, PUBLISHERS
WESTPORT, CONNECTICUT

Originally published in 1953
by The Hogarth Press, London

First Greenwood Reprinting 1971

Library of Congress Catalogue Card Number 71-106715

SBN 8371-3445-5

Printed in the United States of America

To my Wife
who averted the worst

Author's Foreword

Reminiscences seem to me worth telling only if they are truthful. The great Czech statesman President Masaryk was incapable of telling a lie. In a grave situation he preferred the danger of death to a falsehood that might have saved him.

If in moments of excitement I told incredible tales my wife raised her finger in warning and asked, "Masaryk?" If I nodded in agreement, this vouched for the truth.

I have done my best to tell my story in the spirit of Masaryk.

Translator's Note

In this book, *Aus dem Leben eines Musikers*, published in 1949 by the Rascher Verlag, Zurich, Fritz Busch gives a picture of his life till 1933. In that year he left Germany on account of his hatred for the Nazis and his determination never to work with them. He had intended to write a second volume, but his sudden death in 1951 prevented him from completing the story.

On leaving Germany Fritz Busch went to the Colon Theatre, Buenos Aires, where he regularly conducted opera for many years, and also to Scandinavia. In 1934 he came to Glyndebourne. Here, amid beautiful surroundings and with congenial collaborators, he created a unique home for opera, the fame of which soon spread over the musical world. During the second world war his visits to Glyndebourne were necessarily interrupted, and it was during this period that he conducted in the United States, South Africa and other places. After the war he had two more seasons at Glyndebourne in 1950 and 1951, and in the summer of 1951 conducted *La Forza del Destino* and *Don Giovanni* at the Edinburgh Music Festival. Less than a week after the last performance he died suddenly in London.

ERRATUM

Translator's Note
line 16: *for* 'South Africa' *read* 'South America'

Contents

Illustrations

Chapter One

FAMILY AND CHILDHOOD

The friendly throng is scattered.

GOETHE. FAUST. DEDICATION

M Y father was born in the year 1865 at Erndtebrück, a
village in the Westphalian Sauerland. The exact date of
his birth is not certain. His mother told him he entered the
world on July 1st, while in the register of the Evangelical
Church the date is given as July 30th. My father never took
the trouble to clear up this discrepancy. He had no objection
to keeping his birthday twice a year.

My father's parents were peasants who managed a small
farm. But my father had nothing of the peasant in his manner
or appearance. He had dark eyes—I might call them fiery—
delicately cut features and magnificent hair that turned white
early; he had a graceful figure and was agile both mentally
and physically. Instead of taking him for a Westphalian peasant
as he was by descent, one might have supposed his origin to
be quite different. He might have come from Sassmannshausen,
a small place in the neighbourhood where a certain Kurfürst
Moritz had established a settlement of gypsies.

My grandfather fell ill of cancer of the tongue. He was
obliged to go for treatment several times a week to the
University clinic of Marburg, more than forty kilometres
distant. He could not afford to pay for the journey nor to stay
in the clinic, so that he was obliged to go and return each
time on foot. One day it struck him as so absurd to take so
much trouble that he hanged himself in the barn. My maternal
grandfather also committed suicide; we children were never
told why.

As a boy, my father was the village cowherd and to pass

the time he made himself pipes of willow twigs. He loved music and as there was no opportunity in his small village for him to study it he ran away in early youth. In later life he liked to tell stories of the adventurous life he had led for so many years. At the same time he left many episodes shrouded in mystery, which I regret to this day. I am sure that many of them would have been amusing or worth knowing.

In the course of his travels my father went first to Hamburg, where he began to study the violin. As was always the case he did not stay there long, and wandered south with his fiddle. At that time he acquired a remarkable skill, which he retained in later years, of running barefoot across stubble fields. Owing to his restless nature and his dislike of rules and regulations his papers were never in order. Once, at the very moment at which a good-natured peasant woman had given him a plate of hot soup a policeman appeared and asked for his identity card. My father explained readily that he would look for it if the policeman would kindly hold his plate of soup meanwhile. The policeman did so; but my father ran off so quickly that when the good fellow finally made up his mind to put down the hot plate and pursue the runaway he was unable to overtake him.

In his wanderings my father reached München-Gladbach in the Rhineland and there made the acquaintance of a woman twenty years older than himself. He married her, as she had promised him to make it possible for him to continue his musical studies at the Lüttich Conservatoire. This promise was not kept. Instead, the ill-matched pair acquired a small inn at Venlo, a town on the Dutch frontier. My father had meanwhile, goodness knows how and where, learned to play the violin well enough to think he could venture to play the sonatas of Mozart and Beethoven. But he had no pianist. He went in search of one, and at Rotterdam found a Kapellmeister who had reasons of his own for leaving Germany and was on the point of sailing to the East Indies. My father talked him into giving up this adventurous journey and persuaded him to go with him to Venlo. There, in the inn, they industriously played Mozart and Beethoven every day. Whether this music-making discouraged customers, or whether other reasons led to the ruin of the establishment, which soon followed, I do not know. His wife died shortly afterwards, and my father, at about twenty-three years of age, started once more on his travels.

He arrived, thinly clad, and without much luggage, but in possession of a fiddle and a pair of patent leather shoes, at Siegen in Westphalia. There he played one day at a wedding, at the house of good-natured people who invited the musician to eat and drink freely. My father, who must have roused the pity of the holiday-makers by his pallor and thinness, was also bidden to supper in the house of the bride's parents. He sat opposite a girl introduced to him as Fräulein Schmidt, who excited in him the greatest interest. For a long time he stared at his charming *vis-à-vis* with his great burning eyes, without saying a word. She however encouraged him to begin to eat, at which he dreamily remarked, "When I look at you, Fräulein Schmidt, I quite lose my appetite!" It was not poetically expressed, but did not miss its effect, and shortly afterwards a marriage took place between him and Fräulein Schmidt.

My father, who at some time or other had also learnt carpentry, next found a job with a cabinet-maker. At the same time, immediately after the wedding, he got my poor mother to take piano lessons, so that she should be able to accompany his violin-playing as soon as possible. They probably also thought of improving their income by playing dance music together on their free Sundays.

I, their first child, was born in 1890. My mother's capability and industry can be imagined, when one considers that she had eight children, and in the first years of her married life played dance music from Sunday afternoon to Monday morning, while later when we children were somewhat older and could ourselves add to the family earnings, she carried on her own business of embroidery work.

In August 1891 my brother Adolf was born. My mother had been educated with middle-class ideas and wished her children to be christened and brought up as Protestants. My father, who was indifferent about such matters, let her have her way. As, however, he refused to go to church, they agreed to have the baptism of the second child in their own small house. As is often the case where poor people are concerned, the minister did not take much interest in the affair; he had not even taken the trouble to find out the facts about the family. At the last moment he hurried into the house and at once began the baptismal ceremony. "The Lord God," he said, "after presenting this worthy pair with a charming baby boy"—(that was I myself)—"has now filled up the measure of His goodness by bestowing upon them a dear little girl." My mother made horrified signs to the minister. My father smiled with delight. The minister pursued his sermon undeterred till he reached "And now I ask you, dear Parents, what is this girl to be named?" Between sobs and tears my mother broke out, "Adolf Georg Wilhelm." The minister was astonished, but brought the religious ceremony to a rapid conclusion, in order to disappear as quickly as possible.

My mother possessed a keen intelligence together with great good nature and the happy gift of always finding a bright side to the misfortunes and unpleasant experiences which were certainly not lacking in her life. If my father was hot-tempered and of a violent, stormy nature, my mother was thoughtful and patient, so that, in spite of occasional friction, the marriage was a happy one.

It was very soon apparent that we children were musical. My father, besides carpentry and playing dance music, had taken up violin making. I may have been three or four years old when I got hold of a so-called half-sized fiddle, which he had made. I soon, however, preferred to play on a twenty-shilling square piano while Adolf groped his way about on the fiddle, the instrument to which he eventually devoted his life. We learnt to read and understand music very quickly, and at any rate could play easy things at sight long before we could read and write words.

One day a surprising thing happened. My father was taking a walk with Adolf and me when the whistle of an engine was heard. "What note is that?" he asked, and we both instantly answered "F sharp". This immediate agreement was regularly repeated each time my father asked the question on hearing any musical sound. The phenomenon of absolute pitch was unknown to him. He ran, rather than walked, to a distinguished doctor in the town, whom he knew to be a musician. He was afraid that something was wrong with his children, and was only reassured when the doctor explained the situation to him. He learnt that the gift of absolute pitch was to be considered an advantage and not a drawback.

Adolf received his first violin lessons on the above-mentioned small instrument, from my father himself, when he was about three years old. I was four, when an elderly lady came to the house to give me piano lessons. Her fee for an hour's instruction was twopence halfpenny, and she laid out a considerable part of this sum on chocolate and sweets which she gave me at the end of the lesson because she was "so sorry" for me.

In spite of this it would not be true to suppose that the slightest pressure was put on us by our parents to educate us as musicians. My father loved music, and was delighted that his children, at least the two eldest, showed great enjoyment in it. It would never have occurred to him to force us to anything that was not already in our nature and showing signs of development.

His chief anxiety was to find good teachers for us and to let us develop naturally. Without having much education himself but with good instincts he perceived that "if this work be of men it will come to nought, but if it be of God ye cannot overthrow it".

Meanwhile we lived like real street arabs. An inclination towards higher things nevertheless became perceptible. Near our house a railway line crossed the street. The crossing was controlled by an old official who, on the approach of a train, had to raise and lower the barrier. One day Adolf and I, unobserved, tied ourselves fast to the barrier, in order to be lifted with it, sprawling, into the heights. The frightened and angry signalman fetched my father, and . . .

It was some time since my father had given up carpentry and opened a shop for musical instruments, and a workshop for making and repairing string instruments, near the Marburger Tor in our birthplace, Siegen. The shop contained, besides new and second-hand pianos, various woodwind and brass instruments. In the not surprising absence of interested clients, I, for my part, made good use of them. Thus as a child I learnt—literally "in playing"—a great number of orchestral instruments, the practical knowledge of which was later of inestimable value to me. To begin with, as suitable to my size, or lack of it, I took possession of a piccolo with six valves, on which I soon learnt to play fairly fluently.

I was about six years old when I used to accompany Adolf with this flute, as he marched off to another part of the town for violin lessons with a teacher who had taken his diploma at a conservatoire—a thin, lanky, tuberculous youth. As we moved through the town nothing was more natural than that we should produce our instruments—Adolf his fiddle and I the piccolo I always took about with me—and go our way, playing as we went. Opposite the Town Hall, in the market place, in which Peter Paul Rubens was born, we would make our first halt. A great number of boys, accompanied by a few grown-ups with nothing to do, would call on us to strike up, a request that we acceded to only too willingly. On one occasion, after a long performance, when we had played a good many dances and marches, a reasonable man, on the grounds that the labourer is worthy of his hire, thought of organising a collection for us. He went round, hat in hand, and there were actually people who threw in so much small change that we received a concert fee of two marks seventeen pfennigs. Anyone who estimated the musical qualities of our countrymen as critically as we did, must have been most agreeably surprised by this experience. True there were a few buttons among the coins, but we had noticed which boys threw them into the hat, and later settled accounts with them. We joyfully took the money home, sure of meeting with pleased recognition, that we, at such an early age, should have contributed to the improvement of the finances of our ever-increasing family. Our parents, however, felt wounded in their middle-class pride, and we were forbidden in future to carry on the "profession" of music.

I cannot say that my father's shop was a flourishing business. It was especially difficult to sell pianos. If my father in his wanderings found a possible customer in the neighbourhood it enraged him when the future purchaser brought the village schoolmaster along to choose the instrument. This meant not only distrust of my father's honour as a salesman, which would have troubled him very little, but also, when the business was at last concluded, a ten per cent commission for the schoolmaster. We children found this custom unfair, as the musical knowledge of the "expert" did not generally go beyond playing a chorale with incorrect harmonies.

In order not to increase the regrettable loss in the sale by the high cost of transport, my father used to provide himself with a hand truck, which was pulled by the male members of the family, once the instrument was loaded on.to it. I soon found this too laborious. I used to climb onto the truck and play fiery marches, to the delight of the villagers and the amusement of our hardworking family.

Meanwhile I was six years old, and attending the elementary school opposite the post office. The schoolmaster was at the same time commissioned to give me private piano lessons, and I remember beginning Mozart's so-called Sonata Facile with him. But while I continued to experiment with different instruments as well as the piano, Adolf, who dedicated himself entirely to the violin, made more technical progress and was reckoned as a true "infant prodigy".

A choral society approached my father to invite the two children to take part as soloists in a concert which was to end in a ball. In the hall was a small platform on which Adolf made his appearance and played; on the floor of the hall itself was a piano at which I had to accompany him. Adolf played a show piece, *The Carnival of Venice* with a set of variations in A major which got more and more difficult. My piano accompaniment was less interesting; both in the theme and variations it consisted in nothing but broken triads in the tonic and dominant. With such material no personal success could possibly be attained. Consequently, from the second variation onwards I began to exhibit my own skill and to insert into Adolf's passage work some scales in contrary motion, here and there a *glissando* or else some brilliant *fioriture*. Adolf, standing above me with his little fiddle, at first laughed heartily. But when he missed a few notes from lack of concentration he got angry. This stimulated me; my improvisations became bolder and bolder, till Adolf, in a rage, shouted out "Stop it!" As even this was useless he ceased playing, jumped on top of me as I sat well below him at the piano, and beat me over the head with his bow, accompanying his blows with words in the local dialect which could only be reproduced in a paraphrase. Instinctively adopting the attitude of "an eye for an eye, a tooth for a tooth", I on my side jumped acrobatically on to the stage, and a fine bout of fisticuffs began. My father had to rush up hastily and put an end to the scrimmage to the great amusement of the audience. The curtain fell soothingly in the middle of this scene, and we were sent to bed.

Nowadays we settle our differences in a more intellectual fashion.

As the *Carnival* was the last piece in our programme, we had before this been able to show so much musical knowledge that next day a press notice appeared foretelling for us both a future full of promise. In this way, my teacher, Herr Schmidt, discovered that I had "made a public appearance" without his knowledge. My father had neglected to tell him of it and I experienced the full weight of his anger when I went to him next day for my lesson. The *thaler* which my father had given me to pay for some lessons, he flung at my feet, and at the same time flung *me* out of the house. Misfortunes seldom come singly. In deep distress I betook myself from his house to the churchyard opposite, where we used to play with the skulls. I wept despairingly, chiefly because my teacher had refused to take his fee. This seemed to me really terrible. Not so to my father, who pocketed the *thaler*, remarking, "If he doesn't want it let him do without."

More than thirty years later I received a letter from this teacher asking me for a testimonial to say he could give good piano lessons. I gladly sent my teacher this certificate, without which, in consequence of a new law, he would not have been entitled to teach music.

Her household duties and continued pregnancies made it impossible for our mother to go on playing accompaniments from Sunday afternoon to Monday morning in smoky peasants' taverns. My father found no one to help him out. So it happened that one Sunday when I was seven years old I went with him for the first time to Welschenhennest, a small village in Sauerland, to play dance music professionally. With a few interruptions and variations which I shall mention later, these musical performances for money lasted to my seventeenth year—that is for about ten years. During all this time I spent hardly one Sunday or Sunday night at home. Later Adolf took part in these enterprises, though not so frequently. They were often very fatiguing, especially when the playing was followed by many long hours of walking if transport chanced to be lacking; but we never had any dislike of our job of co-operation or any sense of compulsion. For it was *music* we were concerned with, and what sort of music did not at first matter. Of music we could never have enough.

As our proficiency increased we naturally became able to make the whole thing less monotonous.

As soon as I could stretch an octave I continually doubled

the bass and so acquired an excellent technique in the left hand of jumping on to the right notes. I soon knew the repertory by heart, and consequently put on the piano a book by Karl May,[1] which I read while I played polkas, waltzes and country dances.

One day Willi, my parents' third child, came to us, seven- and eight-year-olds, to tell us he too had decided to become a musician. Adolf and I unanimously explained to him that he was too late. He took our advice and later became a "mere" actor.

With time my artistic ambitions grew, and as a future conductor I began to think of producing orchestral effects on a larger scale.

In addition to the piano, which was entrusted to me, there was Adolf with the violin and my father with the 'cello, which he had taught himself to play and had mastered in an elementary fashion. In my right hand I held a cornet on which I played while my left hand alone undertook the piano accompaniment. From time to time a triangle was delicately fitted in. This instrument I fastened to the right-hand candlestick.

Although the time during which we led this life passed without doing us any harm (as far as one can judge of this oneself) and in memory appears only as amusing, I must add that these were very hard years. After leaving the elementary school at the age of ten I went to the secondary school of my home town. Sunday, which for the other pupils was a day of rest after their tiring lessons, was no day of rest for me. As a rule it meant setting out early in the morning on bicycles, by train or on foot, and journeying into the hilly neighbourhood, regardless of wind and weather. We began playing in the afternoon at four o'clock and went on pretty well without stopping till three or four in the morning, and then, thoroughly tired out, began the journey home. At eight o'clock I was once more on my bench at school. I know that my small hands often trembled from over-exertion and that in particular the little finger of my left hand was often really painful from accentuating the bass notes.

[1] Favourite writer for the young.

It does not say much for the intelligence of my teachers, that with hardly any exceptions they were unaware of my double life and my consequent weariness of mind and body. I cannot recollect that the school authorities ever raised any objections or made any complaints. Perhaps they realised that I enjoyed the whole thing and that I was already a victim to music, beyond recall. Besides that my school lessons were easy to me, in spite of my strong musical interests. In those subjects in which I made little progress the fault was in the teaching. I am not exaggerating. With me everything depended on whether a teacher could or could not arouse my interest. I believe that really gifted teachers are as rare as first-class musicians.

Once a year Bohemian street musicians—a band of about eight men in shabby blue uniforms—used to come to our town of 20,000 inhabitants, all thirsting for music, and perform to them marches, *potpourris* and other *pièces*, on trumpets, horns, trombones and tubas. To us the arrival of this band was a familiar event. Their most successful number was "The Post Horn in the Wood". The main body of the band stationed itself in the market-place, by the war memorial, while the first trumpet went off to take up his position about a hundred yards away. The band played a sentimental piece in six-eight time, in which were some post horn calls, which the trumpeter repeated from a distance, as an echo, to the astonishment and delight of the listeners.

Adolf proposed to bring into action a second echo. With this object we hid ourselves far from the band and opposite the position of the echo player. Quite familiar with the music and the general situation, as he played his last note I blew a second echo. In this diabolical fashion I disturbed every entry of the gallant musicians, who, entirely at sea, no longer knew which echo to answer. Finally they broke off, and began furiously to search for the offender. While I, completely absorbed in my musical exercise, was waiting for the moment of my entry, Adolf had been excitedly observing the effect of the double echo. Suddenly he yelled out "Fritz, they're coming!" We rushed to the nearby wood, and hid ourselves there till the danger had passed.

Once more we had moved to another house. My father could never stay in one place for long, and he was always trying to improve his workshop. This time he took a whole house, and let the attics to two boarders, very queer customers. One, a shoe-maker, was a devout Catholic and a quiet self-contained person, while the other was a house-painter, or rather, as he called himself, an "artist". Besides that, he explained to us horrified boys, he was a Social-Democrat. If he had said that he was in the habit of eating small children twice a year our terror could not have been greater. From this vivid recollection I conclude that our father—the political oracle of the family—felt himself a member of the middle classes, for whom Social-Democrats were the worst sort of black sheep. During the latter years of our youth his views developed in a somewhat contradictory manner.

Our two boarders had found regular employment in the town. While the shoe-maker read serious Catholic works in his free time, the painter had taken it into his head to paint a madonna on whom he bestowed fiery red hair. This was eagerly discussed and disputed and the whole family took sides excitedly over the problem.

My father had a great fondness for song birds, chiefly thrushes, chaffinches and robins, which he kept in innumerable cages in the workshop. In a large meal chest there were meal worms which were made use of to feed the birds. Our new house had, to our great delight, a wooden shaft with a lift, worked by pulling a rope and going from ground level up to the workshop under the roof. Near the lift was a speaking tube. We were hardly installed when Adolf ran upstairs to try out this speaking tube. I stood at the bottom, and Adolf called out, "Fritz, just sing *Ah* very loud!" I sang "A-a-ah" and suddenly felt a violent pricking in my mouth. At the top of the speaking tube Adolf had thrown down a handful of meal worms. That night he went to bed rubbing himself, in considerable pain.

Ever since our birth our grandmother had lived in the house with us. She was fondly attached to us children, chiefly occupied in looking after us and the household; her life of effort and toil was precious to us all. She was small but strong, with magnificent blue, piercing eyes. My father, her son-in-law, could not bear her. If he could play her a mischievous trick you could be sure the opportunity would not be lost. His great namesake, Wilhelm Busch, says, "From days of old all people tell, Where there are cares there's drink as well." Certainly my good grandmother had cares enough, on the other hand drink was in general lacking. My father, never very tidy or careful, used to leave the different bottles of lacquer needed for his violins all over the house. One day, worried by her cares, Grandmother seized a bottle and, thinking it contained liqueur recently provided to celebrate some special occasion, took a good pull at it. She gave a fearful scream and presented a pitiful appearance, for the red lacquer was running out of her mouth. My father hurried up to her and explained that the lacquer was poisonous and that Grandmother was lost unless preventive measures were taken immediately. I can still see the old lady, sitting in a chair, pale as death, while my father, a piece of rag in his right hand and the tip of her tongue in his left, rubbed her tongue with spirit. But such accidents did not really disturb the harmony of our family life. On the contrary they only contributed to add colour to it.

When my father had perfected himself in the technique of violin-making, like practically all violin-makers—who must surely have a screw loose—he went in search of the secret of Stradivarius. He was, so to speak, possessed by his work. Once he had begun work on a new instrument he forgot to eat and drink. Hardly had he gone to bed—late enough—than he jumped up again, brewed himself some strong coffee, and ran to the workshop to potter about once more. When various possibilities that might put him on the track of the secret had been tested in vain he suddenly thought he had solved the problem in this way: the back and front of the violin must be tuned to a perfect fifth. We would have let him do as he liked, and the thing would have been harmless enough if my father had known exactly what a perfect fifth actually was. But even then he would not have been sure, from tapping the wood, that he had actually fixed the correct interval. Hardly were the back and front ready when he began, often in the middle of the night, to strike the wood. As he was never certain of the result he used to wake up Adolf and me, who had to go to the workshop in night-shirts and bedroom slippers to verify the perfect fifth. The wood was worked according to our opinion, and he would be satisfied only if we both told him he had got it right. At first we had undertaken the business out of good nature and affection for our father with whom it was difficult to be seriously angry; but in the long run the whole thing appeared too stupid and wearisome. We therefore agreed to say at once, next time, that the interval was D to A, so that we could go to bed and have our sleep. Thus in early childhood we acquired the idea of a white lie to which even grown-ups are sometimes obliged to resort. When at last the fiddle was ready, the family was assembled, and my father, with a trans-figured countenance, drew his bow across the open strings and played an easy passage. On no account did he wish for a sincere criticism. If we had offered one, he would immediately have run back to the workshop to continue his work day and night without rest; or he would have smashed the instrument into a thousand pieces, lamenting bitterly that he was the most useless of God's creatures, and would never in this world bring anything to a satisfactory conclusion. So we poured out praise, and declared that the fiddle was the best he had ever made, with such quality in the workmanship and tone that the instrument was in no way inferior to an old Italian one. Thereupon coffee and cake were produced and the event celebrated. My father disclosed to us—Grandmother, Mother and the more or less grown children—that henceforth all material care for the future was removed; he would sell the fiddle for not less than five thousand marks, even if he had to wait some time for a favourable opportunity; the money should be applied in the first place to our further education; but enough would remain over to fulfil some personal wishes of my mother. At this moment he was even ready to promise something to his mother-in-law.

For a few weeks relative quietness reigned in the house, and our daily life, which had been disturbed by my father's restless activity, went peacefully on its way. We went to school, my father sat in his shop and endeavoured to sell one or other of his instruments, or made small repairs, and my mother busied herself in her embroidery shop which incidentally was enjoying much more custom.

One morning very early my father disappeared out of the house without warning. He had taken with him the fiddle that was not to be sold for less than five thousand marks, to see if he could not manage to dispose of it, even if he had to allow a small discount. It was late in the evening when he came back. What he brought with him was a canary, a walking stick with a crook which he maintained was made of ivory, and a drop too much. He had been to all the different restaurants and cafés where there was music, had also visited individual musicians and offered them a glass of wine and had finally let the precious instrument go in exchange for what I have mentioned above. The canary moreover turned out to be a female, and in spite of every encouragement could never be induced to sing.

When we showed some disappointment my father explained that nothing much could be expected of the instrument; the G string did not ring as it should, had not as much tone as the other strings, and besides the violin had a *wolf* in it. (This is a certain hollow sound which occurs in many instruments, I don't know for what reason, and is very difficult, generally impossible, to get rid of.) Further explanations which he produced very skilfully finally silenced our objections. My father began to construct a new violin and the old game started over again. However, some of his instruments were really very good and for many years Adolf played one of his violins in all his concerts, until he came into the possession of a Stradivarius.

One morning while we were still at the elementary school, Adolf and another boy ran into each other in the playground so violently that Adolf fell down and was in such pain that he could hardly get up. His right arm dangled uselessly in front of him, and the master ordered me to go home with him at once. My parents' alarm can be imagined; not so easily perhaps, the pride with which I announced to my friends on my return to school that my brother had broken his arm. But when later I saw Adolf in bed, bound up in plaster of Paris, the sight terrified me so much that I gave a loud scream and could hardly be pacified. I imagined that my brother would never recover, never be able to play the violin again, and I was not to be comforted.

A doctor put matters to rights cleverly with no after effects. My family was astonished that I was capable of such strong emotion; in general we were not soft and any display of feeling by us was not regarded favourably. They perceived, however, that I was genuinely anxious, and for a few days treated me with forbearance.

My father was continually on the search for a good piano teacher from whom I could really learn something. What he found was not of much value. I remember a little old man who, God knows why, called himself a *Musikdirektor*. But though I never heard a note of music from him, nor a single remark about mine, on the other hand the silent *Musikdirektor* painted harmless little pictures in oils while I played Czerny's studies and Chopin's mazurkas.

I do not remember that this "teacher" or the majority of his successors ever gave me any instruction which I felt to be right and therefore worth remembering. A wretched state of affairs for a boy longing to learn and full of interest. No slick sight reading could conceal the fact that valuable time was

26

being wasted, and in spite of the undoubted ease with which I could have learned, nothing of any value came of my lessons.

By a miracle a chance of help seemed at hand. My mother was a passionate lover of the theatre. Naturally there was at that time hardly any opportunity in Siegen of satisfying her longing for good acting; but once a year a travelling company of actors came to our town. In consequence of the rarity of their appearance they enjoyed greater popularity than they would have deserved in themselves. Their productions greatly resembled in artistic merit those which had made Striese, the theatre manager, into an immortal German comic figure. In order to increase the attraction the director's daughter, who at the same time played the young heroine, sang opera arias in the interval such as "Once my cousin had a dream",[1] or the song by Loewe "Wherever I go I carry my watch".[2] They once gave *The Trumpeter of Säckingen* in a melodramatic version—a work which cannot be properly performed without the co-operation of a trumpeter. I took the part of the performing stage trumpeter, for no one else could be found who was willing to play "Farewell, farewell, how sweet it would have been", standing in the wings at the afternoon and evening performances, in exchange for two free tickets in the gallery.

The orchestra consisted of a worn-out piano "under the direction" of an apparently half-starved individual with sentimental eyes, long hair falling over his collar, and an artist's necktie. This is what we named the so-called *Lavallière*, a broad bow of soft silk with floating ends. Besides this the Kapellmeister—as he was called on the programme—wore a velvet coat and thus presented the ideal artist as I had dreamt of him. My enthusiasm for him increased when my father declared he was *nervy*. Now my aim was fixed. I wanted to be like him, pale, with long hair, an artist's tie, a velvet coat and . . . *nervy*.

[1] Einst träumte meiner seligen Base. *Der Freischütz*, Act III.
[2] Ich trage, wo ich gehe, stets eine Uhr bei mir.

27

My father made his acquaintance, and found that he had studied the piano and violin at the Leipzig Conservatoire. He thought he had found in Kapellmeister G. the right man who was needed in our house to take our musical education into his hands, yellow though they were from cigarette smoking. He was given a room, a little pocket money and free board, and in exchange now and then gave us a music lesson. On the violin his favourite piece was the Adagio from Viotti's twenty-second violin concerto.

About this time my father was driven by vanity to give a concert at Erndtebrück, the town of his birth. My worthy grandmother sat in the box office and invited the peasants to buy "monograms". She was, as you see, not sufficiently good at Greek, so that the confusion between *programme* and *monogram*—a word with which my mother's embroidery shop had acquainted her—was pardonable.

Amongst the various items in the concert a waltz, *Greeting to Erndtebrück*, by my father, deserves special mention. When trying out a fiddle he had improvised a few bars on the G string, which seemed to him an original musical idea. With that, however, his creative powers were exhausted, and *we* had to expand the theme, which was not more than four bars long, to a phrase of eight bars, and add to it. Adolf and I quickly added a few other passages, and wrote a 'cello part for him which of necessity was both beautiful in sound and at the same time technically easy. *The Greeting to Erndtebrück* was ready to perform. The success of the concert was, however, no more than moderate; it was only at the ball which followed that the hall was so full that our efforts turned out not to have been completely in vain.

Next day my father wished to visit Prince von Wittgenstein who lived in a castle at Berleburg, about fifteen kilometres away, and exhibit our powers to him. It was summer, the road was dusty and the journey on foot exhausting. My father, heated like us by walking and standing about, marched into the courtyard of the castle and asked whether we might play to the Prince. He was deeply hurt when entrance was denied us, and declared that the Prince and the united German nobility were conceited ignoramuses, and swore that he was now firmly resolved to follow Bebel's red flag. Death to the aristocracy!

On the way back to Siegen it was decided to repeat our concert and ball in every village with two churches. This would appear to give a guarantee of a sufficiently large music-loving audience. But this artistic tour had an unforeseen end, as Kapellmeister G. suddenly went on strike. He declared that he had not starved for years in order to be able to complete his studies at the Leipzig Conservatoire only to be made use of as a street musician and dance fiddler. When he arrived home, he wrapped up his artistic tie and velvet coat in a cardboard box, was given some bread and butter and other provisions for the journey by my mother, and went off. If I am not mistaken he soon got an engagement at the Darmstadt state theatre, and later made a name for himself as a capable opera conductor.

We had an uncle, my mother's brother, living and working at Duisburg-Hochfeld. He was the pride of the family and especially of my grandmother. By good conduct and strict fulfilment of his duties he had risen from a private soldier in the Berlin guards to be a sergeant-major, and after serving for twelve years had become commissioner of police in the above-mentioned Rhenish town. I think he was at bottom a really typical member of the middle classes, though only too much convinced of the excellence of his own personality and the importance of his position. He was Adolf's godfather, and, proud of his small nephew's performances, constantly went out of his way to introduce him as an infant prodigy to his friends and acquaintances. One day, urged on by his uncle, Adolf played to the then leader of the Duisburg state orchestra, who was an excellent violinist and had the unusual name of Schweinsfleisch.[1] As he would have found it difficult to get on

[1] Hogsflesh.

with such a name he changed it to *Anders*.[1] Mr. Anders, who later became leader of the Cologne orchestra, gave Adolf a few lessons and introduced him to Kommerzienrat[2] S.S., the owner of a wholesale coffee business, who was a millionaire and childless. Impressed by Adolf's talent, he declared he would undertake his further education. My father, to whom we were all alike "dear children", and who could not imagine the possibility of separating the two brothers, calmly expressed the wish that his son Fritz should share these advantages. This, however, was refused. I for my part resisted the scheme. I wished for no patronage. So that when, a little later, Mr. S.S. offered to extend his friendly offices to me I begged my parents to keep me at home, which they did.

Adolf himself, when about eleven years old, entered the Conservatoire of Cologne and was at first the pupil of the eminent violinist and teacher, Willy Hess, who for many years had been the leader of the Boston Symphony Orchestra. For his further education he was placed in the family of a grammar school master. There, by the wish of his patron, who wanted to keep some control over my brother's development, he was to have private tuition in grammar and science. My father, who knew Cologne well from his former travels, took Adolf there himself, and allowed me to go too.

He had always told us of the size and beauty of Cologne Cathedral; in my lively imagination I pictured the building as something prodigious, compared with which everything I had seen before would seem meaningless and insignificant. We crossed the bridge over the Rhine and tried to get a glimpse of the wonderful building. But my father declared this was not the way to do things. The Cathedral must come suddenly upon us, in all its grandeur. Our excitement grew all the more when on reaching the main station our father bandaged our eyes. He led us by the hand across the cathedral square, placed us solemnly in front of the west door, took off our bandages and waited

[1] Another.
[2] A title given to important men of commerce.

eagerly for our impression. I said "Is that all?" and received the one and only box on the ear he ever gave me. His disappointment was too great.

The distance between Siegen and Cologne was also too great, since our Adolf of whom we were so fond had to live alone with an unknown, chilly family who—as it soon turned out—were only intent on making money. Such a long parting at so great a distance was unthinkable to us all; we always felt the need of being able to make close personal contact. It was therefore decided to leave the town of Siegen and to start a new existence at Siegburg in the neighbourhood of Cologne. It was in 1902 that my father's instrument business and my mother's embroidery shop were sold up. By economy, industry and ability, my mother had not done badly in her shop. Together with the receipts from our musical activities there should have remained over from the proceeds of the sale or winding up of the business a few thousand marks.

The winding up was entrusted to a pettifogging lawyer who had been recommended to my parents as particularly capable.

Whatever characteristics my parents may have had they were far from being suspicious. They were both open-hearted and always took for granted that other people were decent and honourable. The day before we were to leave our home town for good and all and the man with the money was expected, he failed to appear. He had disappeared into the blue with the whole of the cash with which we were to start a new life in Siegburg. Of course we never heard of him again. The capital got together by all our hard work was lost. If I am not mistaken, my mother told me some time later that the man ended his days in a lunatic asylum.

His delinquency was a hard blow for us all. Both my parents had wished that I should stop playing for money, go in peace to the Siegburg grammar school, and two or three times a week make the twenty-five kilometre journey to Cologne where I could continue my musical education. My father thought that he would not meet with any competition in the sale of musical instruments in his new residence and would do better business than before, and my mother, in spite of her eight children, wished to open another shop which should really lay the foundations of our new existence. Instead of that, owing to the cheating lawyer, the numerous family would again have to be supported for the time being by the music-making of the father and his eldest son, this time without Adolf.

In 1902 we moved to Siegburg. The little town had at that time about fifteen thousand inhabitants and contained more than two churches, so that the conditions for organising concerts were fulfilled. The place was chiefly notable for a munitions factory on the outskirts. The majority of the people were more military minded than we had been used to in Siegen. Another difference was that Siegburg, lying near Cologne, a centre of Catholicism, was Catholic and strictly controlled by the clergy.

I went to the grammar school where preference was given in the curriculum to Greek and Latin, while in Siegen modern languages had been required. Without any special difficulty I entered the fourth form, at twelve years old. The chief attraction for me in the Siegburg grammar school lay not in the quality of the instruction given but in a little garret directly under the roof. Somebody who knew of my musical interests had told me, a few days after my arrival, that Engelbert Humperdinck, the composer of *Hänsel and Gretel*, was born there.

It was not long before I climbed up under the roof with a few schoolfellows to inspect the room. It proved to be a lumber-room in which, God knows how or why, a large number of battered and dirty wind instruments were lying. The Head Master was a clever and high-minded man, whom I can picture clearly to this day, and who was without question the most valuable member of the staff. With his permission I took possession of the instruments in order to bring them into good repair with the help of my father and one of the assistants whom he sometimes employed for such work. I

Fritz's parents, Wilhelm and Henriette Busch

picked out not more than a dozen boys who were ready to learn the trumpet, bugle, trombone and tuba and who brought to the task some talent and interest. In the course of a few weeks we had learnt to play some Catholic chorales, and could take part in the Corpus Christi procession by performing "Maria zu lieben" and other hymns. In this way we earned the favour of the priests and consequently of the teaching staff, who up till then had looked on our musical efforts somewhat askance.

There was however one teacher, Professor W., who could never endure me. I, for my part, disliked his chilly expression and sarcastic nature. He taught mathematics, and at once realised that I not only had not the slightest gift for this subject, but, which is generally the same thing, was completely lacking in interest and industry. How I managed to bluff my way into the top classes without the smallest effort or knowledge of the subject and without getting into serious difficulties remains a mystery to me. My orchestra meantime made progress; its repertory increased and we were present at all the school celebrations and excursions, at which we were received with applause or indulgence.

Fate willed that one day—whether from rage with me or some other cause—my hated mathematics master suddenly gave up the ghost. When we met in our form room for lessons we were told that Professor W. was dead and that we were to be present at his funeral on the next day but one at a certain hour.

"Good Heavens!" I sighed; meaning really "Thank Heavens", for a large stone had fallen audibly from my heart. Whoever his successor might be he could not be worse.

My chief interest in the circumstances was in the question whether anything to my personal advantage could be extracted from this event—doubtless regrettable in itself. So in the first break I went to the good-natured and somewhat easy-going *Ordinarius*[1] of our class to whose two sons I gave piano lessons

[1] Form master.

free of charge, in order to make clear to him with much eloquence that it was impossible for Professor W. to be buried without music, that is to say without the school orchestra. I was immediately given a holiday until the funeral in order to compose a Dead March and teach it to my friends in the scanty time that remained.

I ran home into the arms of Adolf, who once again, suffering from home sickness, had slipped away from Cologne to play Grieg sonatas with me—they were new to us and we were mad about them. Unfortunately for me Adolf declared he would take part in the composition, and wished to undertake the Trio.

Unfortunately for me, I say, for as usual he overestimated the capacity of his musical contemporaries. He was already playing in the big symphony concerts given by the Cologne orchestra at Gürzenich,[1] knew Wagner as well as Richard Strauss, and therefore did not omit to introduce into his Trio daring harmonies and complicated polyphony which I had wisely neglected in the first part of the Dead March. Uncompromising as he is, he was not to be persuaded to alter it and make it easier. My representations that my boys of the fifth and fourth forms could not possibly play such modern music made no impression. He was particularly proud of a bold piece of counterpoint which he had entrusted to the tenor horn. For nothing in the world would he renounce it. However he agreed to play it himself and with this object he would learn to play the tenor horn in two days. I was so vexed with him that I was mischievous enough not to paint clearly to him the results which were to be foreseen.

"The writing still fresh and the ink still wet,"[2] we went off late in the afternoon to the school hall with my cornet, Adolf's horn, and the manuscript of the other parts. In Adolf's part I had written over every note the crook he was to use.

Never were composers so disappointed as we when the rendering of our Dead March began. It certainly did not sound

[1] A famous Guild Hall in Cologne, where important concerts took place.
[2] "Ganz frisch noch die Schrift und die Tinte noch nass" *Die Meistersinger.*

beautiful. But we were now obstinate, and began to study the work group by group with my "Philharmonic" players, in the hope of still seeing our efforts successful in the end.

Late in the evening two masters appeared in the hall, commissioned by the Head Master to report on the state of affairs. One of them gave singing lessons, the other was a young philologist with a musical turn, of whom more will be said later. Our astonishment knew no bounds when a boy in the top form, the oldest and tallest among us, who played the tuba and had taken part industriously in our long, fatiguing hours of practice, suddenly stood up. He came from the neighbourhood of Siegburg, and boarded with the dead professor's family. Turning to the teachers, he declared laconically that he had been commissioned by Professor W.'s widow to inform us that it had been the last wish of the deceased that Busch and his band should *not* accompany him to the grave.

As already mentioned, the boy who made this crushing announcement was in the top form, and a good deal stronger than the rest of us. And besides he was in possession of the tuba against which it was impossible for us, with our lighter instruments, to struggle.

Adolf and I slunk off home in distress. On the way we discussed whether we could not destroy the boy from the top form so that we could at least play our Dead March at *his* funeral.

On the following Sunday a men's Choral Society in the neighbourhood were celebrating their anniversary, and had engaged the "Busch Chamber Orchestra" to take part at ten marks a man. There were to be ten musicians and it was an advantage for us that Adolf had not yet gone away. What I had expected when I let myself in for trusting him with the horn which he had never touched before, had actually come to pass. The day after we had rehearsed our Dead March his lips were so swollen that he could hardly speak, and he looked more like a native of the Libyan desert than a member of our family of artists. He cursed as loudly as his organs of speech

35

would permit, while I defended myself and put the whole blame on his accursed, senseless imitation of Strauss.

But like everything else this mouth trouble had its bright side. Adolf took it as an excuse for staying at home for a week, and naturally joined our expedition. Our brother Willi would not stay away. He had made various attempts at learning the violin, which had not resulted in our taking him into our band. But now, if Willi could join us, we might make another ten marks—a sum that we could at that time put to a very good use, for we had to be careful of every penny. Adolf and I agreed to take Willi with us, but on condition that his violin bow should be smeared with soap so that none of his disgraceful scraping should be audible.

Willi's desire to take part in the enterprise was greater than his pride. On Sunday morning we prepared for the four hours' walk, ten men strong.

The concert began at six in the evening. The men's chorus, formed by music-loving villagers, and according to custom conducted by the schoolmaster, sang "Dear home, once more I greet thee", and other elevating pieces. Adolf and I had great pleasure, as always, in noting that in the course of the performance the choir had fallen more than a semitone.

But on our side, too, certain concessions had to be made, without which we should have gone hungry—the swindle over Willi, and the star-turn of the programme—Adolf's solo *The Singing Bird*. With this all artistic ideals were abandoned. It was in polka time and I had provided it with an accompaniment that could be altered according to which instruments were available. There was a trio section where the soloist, to the folk tune "All the birds are there", had an opportunity of imitating the chirping of birds with harmonics on his fiddle. Effective passage work, that sounded much harder than it was, led to a brilliant conclusion culminating in such applause from the country people as we could never have attained with better music. This *Singing Bird* was always our last hope when we felt that our other musical efforts were not receiving suitable recognition, and when a second engagement appeared doubt-ful.

Well, Adolf stood on the platform in a blue sailor-suit and short socks. Around him sat the other musicians, I at the piano with my cornet in my right hand, while Willi, more or less concealed in a corner, scraped away with his soapy bow. All the same he felt that he, too, was a member of a "cele-brated" family and on that account was not inclined to hide his light under a bushel. His talent for acting was already excited, and as he knew the music very well he imitated Adolf's violent movements with great zeal.

Two plump ministers were standing in front of the platform, much interested and thoroughly enjoying themselves, and I overheard the following conversation:

"This boy has it in him," said one, looking at Adolf. "*He* has music in his bones."

"Yes," said the other, pointing to Willi, "but it seems to *me* the little one in the corner is the most gifted."

At a big kermesse, which was held in the neighbourhood of Bonn and lasted three days and three nights, the trio—my father, Adolf and I—worked alone to make as much money as possible. As Willi always wanted to be of the party the percussion was handed over to him. But his performance on the big drum with cymbals fastened on to it was disappoint-ing. With the mistaken idea of a ten-year-old that the more noise the better, he accompanied every strong beat of the dance with a loud bang on his unmanageable instrument. We had expected more refinement in a member of our family and did not spare our reproaches. He burst into bitter tears, and lost the spontaneity so necessary to the interpretative artist. Certainly he no longer thumped so much on the strong beat, but in his excitement he made so many wrong accents on the light beat that we had to stop.

But we had not dragged the big drum twenty kilometres with such labour merely to leave it unused. I therefore tied a string to Willi's right arm and made it fast to my left arm.

Willi was earnestly admonished to thump only when I pulled the string.

On another occasion when we arrived at a hitherto unknown village to play dance music for a kermesse, it turned out that there was no piano. This was not much of a misfortune; I played the trumpet and we had with us a double-bass, so that combined with two violins the piano for once was not missed. A worse piece of luck was that the roof came so low over the gallery where we had to sit that the double-bass could not be placed in an upright position. It was a puzzle to know what to do for the best. After some consideration my father decided to climb on to the roof, remove some of the tiles, and push the neck of the double-bass through the hole. During the evening I felt tired and my eyes smarted from the tobacco smoke which permeated the room. I therefore went out into the village street to breathe a little fresh air. There happened to be a full moon. Well on the way to falling into a sentimental mood, while the pertinacious dance rhythm sounded in the distance, I saw five white fingers rising up over the roof of a house—a spectacle which might have excited the imagination of Hoffman.

It is easy to understand that playing on such occasions was extremely hard work. At a kermesse it was usual to make an arrangement with the organising landlord on a piece-work basis. The musicians received no definite fee, but instead half the money taken for every individual dance. While the peasants and their partners took their places, about eight bars of a dance were played and broken off. Someone then went round with a plate into which each gentleman had to throw ten pfennigs; hence this kind of dance music was called *groschen music*. At the end of the collection the money was honestly divided between the landlord and the conductor—in this case, my father—who on his side had to divide his share between his players. If you wanted to get as much hard cash as possible you had of course to play as long as possible, that is to say with the shortest conceivable pauses. This was all the more necessary for us because at my instigation the number of players for this dance music—otherwise so uninteresting to me —was continually being augmented. Clarinets, trumpets, trombones, sometimes flutes and percussion, were brought in, and as many of the performers could play several instruments, I for my part could change about and practise on the various instruments. But each one of them naturally wanted to receive what he had earned, so that we had to redouble our efforts. In the course of the evening the peasants got heated from their unrestrained indulgence in spirits and beer, and it often came to blows. The quieter element then called for music, with the idea that its well-known soothing effects would restrain the quarrelsome lads from throwing beer glasses about or thrashing each other with their sticks. But we were thoroughly experienced and at the cry of "Music!" vanished into the blue. We had, beforehand, as in Haydn's Farewell Symphony, packed up our music and instruments, one after the other, and unobtrusively diminished our numbers until at last only two or three musicians remained and at the end took to flight. It sometimes happened that furious peasants pursued us, and we were afraid we should make acquaintance with their fists. But we were always lucky.

My father had opened a musical instrument shop in Siegburg, with the money we had earned by our playing. He had succeeded in getting a commission to supply a great number of wind and string instruments to start a local orchestra in Prussian Rhineland. One Sunday morning a young peasant came to the shop wishing to acquire a double-bass. They bargained for a long time; the peasant was cautious, slow in making up his mind and not inclined to part with his hardearned *thalers* in an enterprise the value and outcome of which he felt to be doubtful. All of my father's persuasive eloquence was in vain till he had the bright idea of promising the peasant the necessary instruction in how to play the double-bass, if he bought the instrument.

Sitting in the next room I began to turn white and red

when I heard my father, in reply to the peasant's question, explain that the teacher would be his son Fritz. The double-bass was the very instrument in which up till then I had taken the least interest. I had never played the double-bass, or even drawn a bow across one. But there was nothing to be done. To all my objections my father simply declared, "You can play any instrument if you want to." The purchase was made and the following week the peasant appeared for his lesson. In the future half an hour before the lesson I regularly learned from a "Self-teacher for the Double-bass" what I handed on, thirty minutes later, to the peasant. Adolf often helped with this job.

Twenty years later I was the director of the Dresden State Opera. One morning a visiting card was brought to me from someone who, in spite of all the measures taken to keep out unwanted visitors, stuck to it that he must speak to me. On the card appeared: "Karl Knecht. Double-bass and Saxophone. Pupil of Fritz and Adolf Busch." Our work had been rewarded.

The first teacher who was really of use to me was a certain Inderau who conducted a music society at Siegburg. He had attended the Cologne conservatoire and had received a thoroughly good musical and general education. In return for my playing the viola at his orchestral performances or under-taking the high trumpet part in Bach's F major Brandenburg Concerto, Inderau gave me a piano lesson every week free of charge so that I could now prepare regularly to enter the Cologne conservatoire. Adolf's patron allowed my brother to buy the music he wanted at Weber's music shop in Cologne, and Mr. S.S. undertook to pay for it. Adolf made a reason-able use of this generous permission, and amongst other things bought miniature scores of the latest works of Richard Strauss and other contemporary music, as well as Tausig's vocal score of *Die Meistersinger*. Of course I naturally did not let this opportunity slip.

We had the greatest enthusiasm for *Die Meistersinger*, but we preferred the humorous and comic bits of Beckmesser, while Hans Sachs's renunciation at that time left us cold. How much easier it is to remember what one learns in youth than later! I realise this to-day, every time I conduct *Die Meistersinger*. Passages like Beckmesser's song, or the scene in the third act between him and Hans Sachs, I knew by heart perfectly as a boy, while all the rest of the music I only learnt properly later on and had to impress it on my mind with an effort.

Among Richard Strauss's works, *Till Eulenspiegel's Merry Pranks* seemed to us, and seems to me still, the most perfect. I made for myself a piano version of the work, so as not to be disturbed by continually having to turn over the pages of a small score, and was soon able to play the work fluently and with orchestral effect.

Adolf, who at that time was also devoted to the study of composition, was busied with a *St. Mark's Passion* which has unfortunately disappeared from among Bach's works. He hoped to make good the regrettable loss with his own work!

But for a time Richard Strauss overshadowed everyone else, and after we had got to know *Don Quixote* and *Till Eulenspiegel* we resolved to collaborate in a Symphonic Poem on Wilhelm Busch's *Max und Moritz*. I invented the Max theme, in one bar, Adolf the Moritz theme, also in one bar. It opened *vivace* with a C major *glissando* for the harp, then with syncopated open fifths C–G in the first violins both themes appeared and were developed *à la Strauss*. For this composition we had various original ideas which so far had not been made use of in programme music. Thus in the "first prank" in which Max and Moritz cross two threads one over the other and tie pieces of bread to their ends for the well-known poultry trap, this episode, so suitable for musical treatment, also made an optical effect in our score. On one side of the score at the left ran a scale from below upwards, through all the instruments up to the piccolo; at the same time a scale in contrary motion ran from the piccolo above down to the double-basses below on the right.

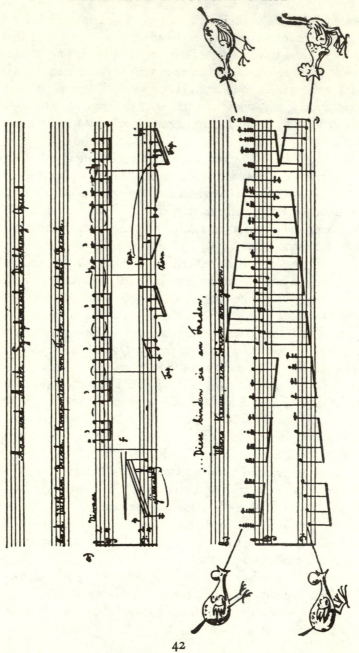

We had progressed successfully in our joint composition as far as the "third prank", in which Meister Lampe plays the chorale in church, while Max and Moritz in his house stuff up his beloved tobacco pipe with powder. This process we depicted by a lively movement in semi-quavers against the *Canto Firmo* of the chorale when a thought struck me which suddenly brought me to a stop. I told my brother that in all probability our work had no sense. Our idea seemed to me so excellent that doubtless it had already occurred to Richard Strauss long since and after *Don Quixote* and *Till Eulenspiegel* he must have turned his attention to a *Max and Moritz*.

Adolf shared my fears. Putting the work on one side we sat down and wrote to *Herrn Hofkapellmeister Richard Strauss* in Berlin, asking him to be so kind as to drop the composition of a symphonic poem, *Max and Moritz*, which he no doubt had in mind, as *we* were already engaged in it. We received no answer. Twenty years later, on the occasion of my first performance of his *Intermezzo*, Strauss called our letter to memory with much amusement.

Naturally my preoccupation with music almost completely annihilated my feeble interest in the curriculum and other school duties. I might perhaps struggle fairly well through the subjects which I enjoyed either from the master's personality or the subject-matter, owing to a certain quickness of understanding and a good memory. But my performances in mathematics and science were so catastrophic that the worst was to be feared. This *worst* was the repetition of a whole school year for which I had no inclination at all. At that time I was in the sixth class. The successful completion of a year's work in this class gave one the right of doing only one year's military service instead of two. To obtain this right was my only object, in order to avoid a waste of time and further hindrances to an undisturbed study of music. The diploma certified that the pupil had passed the preliminary examinations before matriculating. It also gave its possessor a certain social standing as a citizen, in a country where an academic

43

education in any form had more weight than it deserved. This made more impression on my father than on me. It was another proof of his contradictory attempts to adjust himself socially, which gave us growing children occasion for merriment and even for opposition. Since the coffee magnate had interested himself in Adolf, our father actually sympathised with capitalism and once categorically forbade my politically minded sister Elizabeth to follow in the train of the Social-Democratic Youth Party behind the red flag, which he himself had followed in former times.

I knew pretty accurately how I was doing at school and what I wanted. On the other hand I did not know what my teachers thought of the affair. In order to obtain this information I leagued myself with one of the other boys—a real adventurer such as is always to be found in a school, who intended to run away from home as soon as possible and join the Foreign Legion. (Instead of that he later became a Prussian official.)

One sleepy, hot, spring afternoon we broke into the Head Master's study to read our reports which were kept there in the class record books. Just as, in our agitation, we were opening the wrong book the school porter came in and caught us in the act.

My knowledge of human nature was increased when next morning I discovered the reactions of the different masters to our exploit. That of the physics master made the greatest impression on me, when he remarked cynically that he simply could not imagine how I could have embarked on such a risky enterprise. "For, my dear boy," he went on, in the face of the grinning class, "you know quite well that two failures are enough to make a remove impossible. You knew you had two failures and would probably have more. Why then all the excitement?"

How much more powerfully this convincing logic worked on me than the box on the ear from the moustachioed history master. To this fellow, if I had then known what was to happen some thirty years later, I should have prophesied a brilliant career as a Gauleiter.

But amid all my misfortunes one piece of good luck befell me. A short time previously a young philologist had joined the staff, an excellent, clever young man, well-educated and with an unusual gift for teaching. He was the son of a conductor at Bonn on the Rhine, his name was Otto Grüters, and a few years later he became Adolf's brother-in-law. Grüters had followed my musical activities attentively, as well as my academic failures at school, but without saying anything. The kindly Head Master punished me and my intolerable curiosity with a few hours' detention and then resumed his normal relations with me. Then one afternoon Grüters told me to come to his rooms. Earnestly and impressively he declared that it would really be a pity to give up the attempt so few weeks before reaching the goal, the importance of which was unmistakable. He thought it was quite possible for me to pass the final examination if, throughout the last months, I really worked with a will. He was ready to help me.

Next day found me in his room with my algebra and geometry books. He began with a test, going from hard to easier questions, to check up in half an hour on my attainments. A long pause followed, during which he looked thoughtfully out of the window. Then he told me that he was faced with a phenomenon. This was the problem of how anyone could have bluffed his way for four years with this complete absence of knowledge.

I could have given him a few hints which would have been of use to him in his future career as a teacher, but I wisely said nothing.

Grüters decided that he would trust to my memory and adopt a method that he did not at all like; instead of filling up the blanks in my mind with thorough, intelligent work, he got me to master the subject-matter of the examination by *memoria technica*. This was the last expedient, and his method proved to be admirable. I learnt by heart all the formulae and book work, superficially it is true, but quickly and correctly, so that after a few weeks I was at the top of the class, and should have got a brilliant first in the examination if a small mistake had not crept in. I confused the premises of one of the problems with the conclusion, put the conclusion in the place of the premises and used the premises as the conclusion, in this way making the coda the introduction. For "every sin is punished on earth".[1]

Always intent on promoting my general education, Otto Grüters invited me, one holiday, to go with him to Bonn. In that town there was a small privately endowed picture gallery. It contained chiefly pictures of the Dutch School. We stood for a long time in front of a realistic painting, "Judas Iscariot throwing the thirty pieces of silver at the feet of Jesus". As we went away silently and solemnly my mentor suddenly asked: "Fritz, can you be quite truthful?"

After a long pause he received the answer, "I'll try."

"Well then, tell me honestly, what were your feelings while you were looking at this celebrated painting?"

"I was counting to see if the painter had put exactly *thirty* pieces of silver into the picture."

"Thank you. I thought as much."

As preparatory studies for the Cologne conservatoire I had secretly played several times in the school orchestra, smuggled myself into the rehearsals of the Gürzenich concerts and made the acquaintance of Adolf's friends and the players in the Orchestra. Now I wanted to hear the open rehearsal of a Gürzenich concert at which the students of the conservatoire had free admittance to the gallery on presentation of their permits. I felt I was already practically a student, and Adolf kindly put at my disposal the necessary card, made out in *his* name. I travelled in my Sunday best from Siegburg to Cologne, got Adolf's document and reached the gallery without further question. In the programme were Mozart's Jupiter Symphony and Beethoven's Eighth. I was all eyes and ears for the big

[1] "Alle Schuld rächt sich auf Erden." Goethe.

orchestra, tuning their instruments, and was admiring Adolf who, only fourteen years old at the time, was seated at a back desk of the second violins, when the inspector of the conservatoire appeared in the gallery and asked to see my permit. In spite of any family likeness there was no doubt that Fritz was not Adolf. During the opening bars of the Jupiter Symphony I was kindly but firmly sent out, and I do not deny that tears came into my eyes, for it was impossible for me to buy a ticket however cheap it might be. I was not even allowed to stand outside the door and could only inform Adolf of my misfortune through one of the players in the first interval. Next day my kind brother was summoned before the Director for misuse of his permit, but got off with a reprimand.

Shortly before the end-of-term examination the Head Master of the Siegburg school ordered me to come to him. He told me that in consideration of my unmistakable musical gifts, and lack of means, of which he was aware, he had shut his eyes to much, and would now show grace rather than righteousness if I would definitely promise to leave the school after the remove. I jumped as high as the ceiling, and assured him that I had already applied for admittance to the Cologne conservatoire. I was thus able to leave school with the desired certificate.

Of course it would have been impossible for me to attend the conservatoire without the grant of a free place. To obtain this it was necessary to pass a special examination. One summer morning I waited for four hours in an ante-room of the music school. Through the door of the room in which the examination was taking place, I heard violins playing uninterruptedly. At midday some of the professors left the room, and I shyly asked the director's secretary, who was passing, when *my* turn would come. She told me that the remaining violin candidates for free places were to come the following morning. I replied that I played the piano, not the violin. To my horror I now heard that all the free places for that instrument had been given on the two previous days. She, the secretary, had taken it for granted that I played the violin, like my brother. (Why on earth, silly goose? I thought to myself.) If this was not the case I must come back next year.

Was I again to lose the school year I had saved?

I cannot remember how I reacted to this information. In any case the result was that the "typing machine" (as we afterwards called the secretary) went back to the examination room to explain the misunderstanding. There she seems to have adequately described the despairing attitude of "little Busch".

The director of the conservatoire was Fritz Steinbach; his predecessors were Ferdinand Hiller and Franz Wüllner who for his part, on account of the well-known differences of opinion in Munich, replaced Hans Richter as the conductor of the first performances of *Das Rheingold* and *Die Walküre*. These distinguished men had established the fame of the Cologne conservatoire which, together with Leipzig, held the highest place in Germany for music teaching. When Fritz Steinbach became the head of this celebrated establishment a few years earlier he was a man who owed his great fame as a conductor chiefly to his travels with the Meiningen orchestra, as successor to Hans von Bülow. His speciality, so to speak, was Brahms. But he was by no means a one-sided musician.

It in no way affected his position as a big personality and a really great conductor that snobs and unmusical critics often mistook his musical importance and classed him as "military" and "monotonous". It is surely enough that Brahms often said he could not imagine a better interpreter of his symphonies and that Toscanini used to tell me that he had never heard anything more beautiful than certain performances by Steinbach. Once when he was conducting the Haydn Variations in Turin, which Toscanini shortly before had studied and performed with the Turin orchestra, Steinbach asked the players how it was that they were such complete masters of the style of this work. Toscanini considered this praise as among the highest he had ever received.

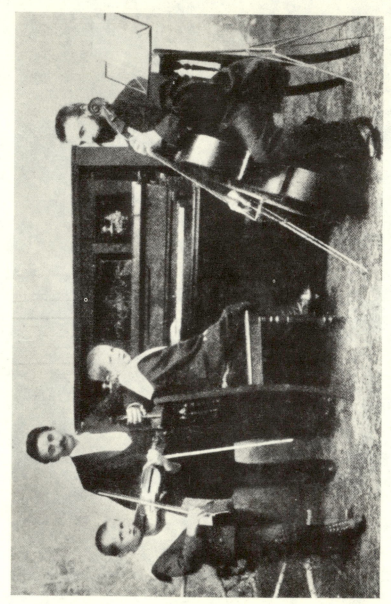

Fritz and Adolf Busch with their father and Kapellmeister G.

Napoleon cannot have been more determined to win the battle of Marengo than I was on entering the examination to win my battle and obtain the endangered free place. My jumpy entrance, my impetuous and excitable manner, the longing clearly shown to reach my goal at any price, aroused the hilarity of Steinbach and the other professors. I played Bach's Toccata and Fugue in C minor. In the middle of the piece they called out "That'll do!" and Steinbach tested my hearing, while I had to stand with my back to the piano, in a corner of the room. He struck a few notes which I immediately named, and thereupon called out crossly and self-confidently, "That's all much too easy! Simply put your arms on the keyboard and I'll name the notes, one after the other." Steinbach then played a chord which I named as F, B, D sharp, G sharp. "Or if you prefer it, F, C flat, E flat, A flat," I added, "and besides, it's the first chord in the Prelude to *Tristan*."

I must have behaved like an intolerable youngster. Luckily they did not take it in bad part. Moreover Steinbach explained that it was true that all the free places had been allocated, but there was still the possibility of admitting me without the payment of school fees if I could learn an instrument for the orchestra. He first suggested the double-bass. Remembering the lessons I had given to Karl Knecht and my considerable experience with this instrument, I replied haughtily, "I know it." When he suggested wind instruments he got the same answer. At that I immediately received for the time being a half-place for which I had to be at the disposal of the school orchestra when required.

For further instruction in the piano I joined Karl Boettcher's class; in harmony and counterpoint that of Professor Klauwell, a clever but somewhat dry teacher. I cannot say that I was pleased with this result. I was anxious to enter Carl Friedberg's advanced class and to become a finished pianist as soon as possible. At any rate the half free place was soon changed to a whole one shortly after I had started my lessons and had played different instruments in the orchestra. In the end I attached myself to the kettle-drums which I shared with Knappertsbusch, later my opposite number at Munich.

I can best describe the character and appearance of my piano teacher Boettcher in the words of Weingartner, who in his autobiography writes at length of this friend of his youth. "Kienzl (the composer of *Der Evangelimann*) had spoken to me of him with such special warmth that I was very curious to make his acquaintance. I was not disappointed. . . . A true German, tall, with a ruddy face and bright blue eyes, he immediately attracted me by his open manner. . . . Then too I felt that I could be really friendly with this man . . . Boettcher, with his fair hair and bright blue eyes, looked like the god Froh in the *Rheingold*. . . . Boettcher had once more drawn the bow of his sarcastic wit and was only waiting to loose his arrows on me, privately and in front of others. . . . My friend Boettcher now had another opportunity to jeer. . . . This led to a temporary estrangement . . . but our friendship was not permanently disturbed. In later life we did not see each other for many years. When we did meet again at Cologne, where Boettcher was a teacher in the conservatoire, we were good friends as of old. We used to sit ourselves down in some corner with a good glass of wine and talk over our past youth, its follies and glories."

Besides Weingartner, Boettcher had also got to know Gustav Mahler and Arthur Nikisch well, in his Leipzig days. He was thus the right man to tell me tales for which I importuned him, from the treasure of his rich and interesting memories in which there was always something new about his relations with these three great conductors. I myself, for many years, long before I had entered the conservatoire, had been firmly resolved to become a conductor.

My interests centred, not in the piano but in the many possibilities of the orchestra. Though I had never seen or heard a good conductor until the moment when Fritz Steinbach crossed my path, I always felt myself instinctively drawn to the widest possible versatility in the field of music and considered the study of the piano only as a means to this end. My father had to make me a conductor's baton, glasses and bottles were arranged in the order of battle of a large orchestra, the score of the *symphonia domestica* was placed on Adolf's violin stand, and the game was ready to begin. Now, in Steinbach, I felt the value of a conductor's personality, which was decisive for my further development.

My progress in the piano under Boettcher was not remarkable, though I practised day and night, because the teacher did not like teaching, had no gift for it, and let himself be taken in by slick sight-reading. But in spite of this I owe him an immense debt for my general development. Boettcher was above all a disciple of Wagner, whose works and writings he knew in the greatest detail, while he considered Brahms, the favourite of Steinbach, with respect but coolness. He had a sincere love of music and everything beautiful, and had a comprehensive knowledge of literature. Thus he opened up to me Goethe and other classics, Hebbel, Ibsen, Russian and French writers, and placed at my disposal his extensive library of literature and piano music. From 1906 to 1909 I studied music to the point of exhaustion and simply could not assimilate enough of it. But at the same time I always carried about a good book with me, which I read with avidity.

After my entrance into the conservatoire my parents also moved to Cologne, where my father hoped to make a living by making violins and repairing stringed instruments. A change of house did not mean much to the family. Up to the time when I left my parents our home had changed fifteen times. It seems to have been written in the stars that I too, in my later life, should never settle down definitely, but be fated to wander restlessly through the world.

By the time we migrated to Cologne the family had further increased. Elizabeth was born, who later, like my brother Willi, went on the stage and continued in this profession till her marriage. Then came Hermann, who early took to the violoncello and to-day plays in my brother Adolf's quartet.

51

A younger brother, Heinrich, also a musician, died very young; he had composed a number of songs, which were pleasing rather than important, and were much sung in Germany. A sister also died at the age of eighteen, and a third, many years earlier, as a small child, so that of their eight children my parents lost three in their youth.

Until the end of our years of study it never entered Adolf's or my head to give up playing to make money for the family. The statutes of the conservatoire naturally forbade playing for money; just as naturally we paid no attention to this prohibition. Only the playing of dance music was put a stop to, and we confined our activity to giving concerts in restaurants, in which as a rule Adolf, myself, another violinist and a 'cellist took part. With a certain amount of friendly diplomacy we had succeeded in persuading my father to allow himself a rest and devote himself entirely to his violin making, so that we could introduce into our quartet an excellent young 'cellist who better fulfilled our musical requirements. We played well and seriously, and the knowledge of light music which I thus acquired was of great use to me.

It is unnecessary to raise the question of the relative value of music. Of course there is a world of difference between Bach's St. Matthew Passion and a waltz by Johann Strauss. The interpretation of the Passion, however, by no means excludes the good performance of a waltz. Reverence for Johann Sebastian should not make a musician deaf to the fact that Johann Strauss's little compositions are miniature masterpieces.

There were some technically skilled and gifted students who felt it inconsistent with their pride to join us in our "strumming" as it might be called. In the long run hardly a single one of these students, who were going about with their noses in the air, came to any good.

How many pianists played Liszt's Concertos and Chopin's B minor Sonata with great brilliance at the conservatoire concerts without being able to accompany a simple Schubert song at sight! We took a different path. If Adolf was not practising the violin he was busied with chamber music or playing in an orchestra. Besides that he composed or helped me with arrangements otherwise unobtainable of the music we needed for our small orchestra. At home we played Bach's organ works as duets, I the manuals, he the pedal in octaves, and in addition, when necessary, he played the viola. I myself was much sought after as an accompanist in singing lessons and in the teaching given by the leading members of the town orchestra to woodwind and brass. While studying piano music on my own behalf I was able, living and making music in the same house as my brothers, to become thoroughly acquainted with the violin, and later violoncello music. To-day I am thankful that in my most receptive years I had the opportunity of acquiring a many-sided knowledge of musical literature, without effort, and always with enjoyment. I was thus able to lay a firm foundation for the profession of my life.

Chapter Two

YEARS OF STUDY

*We are not granted a
second youth.*[1]

THE years I spent in Cologne from 1906 to 1909 were a
happy time. From my own experience I think I can say
that for a student of music a course at a good conservatoire is
preferable to any private teaching. The intercourse with young
people of like interests, the variety of contacts with personalities
of all kinds, the different claims, the stimulus which the curriculum brings with it heighten one's interests. Above all they
favour the critical faculties.

The Cologne conservatoire was full of life. A great number
of foreigners, attracted by the international fame of the institute, were to be found among the students. There were many
Dutch, English and Americans; and even a Basque priest appeared for some days to take part in Steinbach's conducting
class.

Although I was always trying to force my way into the
conducting class I was at first not admitted to it, as at sixteen
I was thought to be too young. Nearly every evening I used to
go to the opera or the theatre with my teacher, Boettcher.
Either before or afterwards we had a meal in his handsome
bachelor rooms. He used to prepare it himself and it was richly
supplied with farm produce sent by his relations in the country.
Boettcher explained that he would have taken a better seat for
the performance if he had been alone, but preferred the cheaper
ones in my company. He was proud of his pupil.

All the harder did he feel the blow that fell after about a
year's teaching. In the yearly examination I played a Beethoven
Sonata and happened to arouse the highest displeasure of

[1] Nicht zweimal wird die Jugend uns zuteil.

54

Steinbach who, as the head of the teaching staff, conducted this examination. There was a reciprocal antipathy between him and my teacher. Boettcher, in his sarcastic, ironical way—in itself opposed to the other's rough, violent temperament—criticised Steinbach's one-sided preference for Brahms and could not manage to keep his criticism to himself. Steinbach not only knew about it, but he saw very clearly that Boettcher, though his general knowledge was comprehensive and included music, was after all neither a great teacher nor a born musician. At every examination, Steinbach, who could be extremely disagreeable, drove me to such despair that I played even worse than I should otherwise have done. For years I suffered from stage fright if I had to appear on the platform to play a piano solo, though I was never aware of the least inhibition when playing with an orchestra or in chamber music.

As I afterwards discovered, Steinbach's criticism—which, though really severe, he was quite entitled to make—was dictated by a definite aim. The Master Class to which I, to my sorrow, had not so far been admitted, was taken by Carl Friedberg with unusual success. Besides him, another teacher had been engaged. This was Professor Uzielli, a pupil of Clara Schumann's, who had given up his position in Frankfurt-am-Main on the condition that at Cologne the best possible students should be assigned to him. The day after the unfortunate examination Steinbach informed me that there was no sense in my continuing to study with Boettcher and that in future I was allotted to Professor Uzielli's class. When I reached Boettcher's rooms that evening I found my teacher and friend much disturbed and in a mood to commit some folly, so great were his grief and rage. Time healed them both, and our lasting friendship was untroubled.

My studies with Uzielli began with weeks of finger exercises to equalise my scale technique, and in this way for the first time—thank heavens not too late—a real teacher gave me a foundation on which I was later able to build on my own account. For the next two years until I left the conservatoire I studied with him and worked like one possessed, so that I acquired a big repertory and could be reckoned a good pianist.

After I had changed over to Uzielli, Steinbach was satisfied, and at the next examination went to the opposite extreme with exaggerated praise. I made use of his friendly mood to ask him again to take me into the conductor's class. After I had played from a score successfully he finally agreed.

There were about eighteen of us students of conducting. Two always played from the score on two grand pianos while the budding Kapellmeister conducted. Apart from brief remarks as to style, phrasing, or the tempo of the work, we hardly received any directions or advice with respect to the technique of conducting.

As it turned out, none of my fellow-students in conducting, with the exception of Hans Knappertsbusch, became Kapellmeisters who were above the average. But this failure was owing to lack of talent and not the fault of the teacher.

Conducting is the art which it is least possible to teach, and the expression "a born conductor" is certainly justifiable. To make a musician into a great conductor too many qualities disconnected with musical powers are necessary, as well as the original musical talent which is naturally the basic essential. There are outstanding musicians who, face to face with an orchestra, fail completely, and very mediocre ones who as conductors produce effects above the average. It is therefore easy to understand that the critics and the public are much more often deceived as to the real worth of a conductor than when judging a singer or instrumentalist. But this subject is, as Fontane says, "a wide field".

Though I could now take part in Steinbach's conducting class, yet the all-powerful, whom we honoured as much as we feared him, did not allow me to demonstrate my powers in front of an orchestra. He thought that at seventeen I was still too young for it and in spite of the remarkable sympathy that he showed me on every sort of occasion he would not alter this decision. His sympathy for me was aroused by the fact that I was always to be found where an orchestra was assembled or any other interesting form of music was being performed. If in a Gürzenich concert or the school orchestra a performer on an instrument that I could play was missing, I was on the spot as a substitute. In order to get to know works that specially interested me in the opera or concert hall I forced my way into the orchestra and, secretly or with the consent of the Kapellmeister concerned, replaced one or other of the tired or absent musicians who willingly surrendered his place to me.

Steinbach's programmes gave the chief preference to classical and romantic music. Above all, as before mentioned, the works of Brahms were regularly performed. Steinbach was also, however, an outstanding conductor of Beethoven, and I have never heard, for example, the Adagio of the Ninth Symphony played with such obviously right tempo, so warmly and tunefully, with such correct phrasing—in a word, in such a convincing manner—as by him. Though Steinbach was in the first place definitely a concert conductor, who had had relatively few opportunities for conducting opera, he possessed a naturally dramatic temperament. Even Boettcher, the Wagnerian, who knew all the important opera conductors of the time and regularly attended the Bayreuth performances, admitted that Steinbach's interpretation of the Dead March from *Götterdämmerung* was one of the greatest experiences of his life.

As was the case in many German towns at the close of the Gürzenich concerts at Easter, there was always a performance of Bach's St. Matthew Passion, the only alternatives being the less popular St. John's Passion or the B Minor Mass. To strengthen the permanent orchestra we members of the conservatoire were often called in. To the average orchestral player this work, with its many pauses and the frequent repetition of chorales, appears tedious. He would rather execute the most difficult passages of Strauss. During the performance the man sharing my desk once whispered to me the old musician's joke, "You know, Busch, this may be Saint Matthew's Passion—it's not mine!" But it was and still is *my* passion.

I learnt to know the language of the orchestra and the psychology of the musician from top to bottom. No study between four walls in a music school or university can take the place of this living education. It contributed substantially to making Hans Richter, Nikisch, Toscanini and other great conductors whom the orchestra itself, the true, expert judge, honoured and loved and will continue to love though occasionally to fear. The conductor must be intimately acquainted with the sorrows and joys, the weaknesses and merits of the musicians. It does not matter with what accent he speaks the language of the orchestra; the straightforwardness of Richter, the insinuating charm of Nikisch, the demoniacal power of Toscanini which goes to the most daring extremes of aggression in every way, lead alike to unusual performances if the conductor, like these masters, speaks the *language of the orchestra*.

In the Cologne Opera Otto Lohse, a very stimulating conductor, was working. He had prepared for performance Weingartner's opera *Genesius* (which the orchestra jokingly called *Gewesius*[1]). The opera was a success, so that the composer was invited to a later performance of it. This was at the time when Weingartner, a conductor of completely different methods from the others, was quarrelling with the Musicians' Union on account of the Munich Kaim Orchestra which he conducted. The musicians, swayed by their prejudices, thus met him with no sympathy when, without a rehearsal, he stepped to the desk to conduct his work. I was extremely excited at seeing with my own eyes this internationally celebrated man, whose portrait had hung in my room for years. I therefore smuggled myself into the orchestra pit into an empty seat next the bass clarinet. Before Weingartner gave the beat he shut his eyes so as to prepare for the right mood of the solemn opening bars. My bass clarinet said in audible tones, "You see, Busch, that's another who acts like everyone else."

On that evening I could get no impression of the work or

[1] Has-been.

the personality of the conductor. It was only future meetings that showed me clearly that Weingartner was a quite excellent musician and a conductor on a great scale. In his prime, which coincided with my youth, the convincing naturalness and simplicity of his conducting made a deep impression on me which remains with me still.

For us conservatoire students the appearance of an important guest conductor, after we had once become familiar with the peculiarities of our own conductors, was of course always an event. Variety is agreeable, and our interest rose to the highest point when the town of Cologne instituted opera festivals with the co-operation of artists from other towns.

In the summer of 1908 Nikisch came to conduct *Die Meister-singer*. I was playing with the percussion, the miniature score in front of me so as not to let the least detail escape me. A certain electric tension which emanates from an expectant gathering had taken possession of the assembled orchestra. It was ten minutes after the time fixed for the beginning of the rehearsal when opposite my seat, on the other side of the orchestra pit, a door opened and a small, very elegantly dressed gentleman came in. He bowed quietly to the nearest horns and greeted them and the other wind players with such charm that when he stepped up on to the conductor's rostrum the whole orchestra were already on their feet, and had broken out in enthusiastic applause. Nikisch took his time, removed his kid gloves, bowing in a friendly way in all directions, and after an introductory silence declared in a pleasant voice that it was the dream of his life to conduct this famous orchestra. He said the same thing, from inborn amiability, wherever he appeared as a guest conductor.

He suddenly interrupted himself, stretched his hand out towards an old viola player, and cried out, "Schulze, what are *you* doing here? I had no idea that you had landed in this beautiful town! Do you remember how we played the *Berg Symphony* under Liszt at Magdeburg?" Schulze did remember it and immediately resolved that with *this* conductor he would use the whole length of his bow instead of playing with only half, as was his custom with the usual conductors.

It was also a speciality of Nikisch to know the players by name quickly and never make a mistake. I felt at once that, before he had even begun to conduct, the hearts of the whole of the orchestra had been won, and that with the first C major chord of the introduction something unusual was to be expected.

The paradox that under Nikisch, when he merely stood on the rostrum the orchestra already sounded better than with other conductors, really proved to be a fact. With sudden energy he raised his long baton, provided with a handle turned on a lathe, and said: "Please, gentlemen; in the first two bars great brilliancy in the brass, then let them retire and give the precedence to our splendid strings."

The up beat and the down beat followed. The first bars, with the somewhat sticky orchestration through which the quavers of the violins in the second bar are so often hardly perceptible, were immediately heard, solemn and clear. After a few bars it seemed as if one were listening to a completely new work. In the course of the rehearsal Nikisch spoke very little, and skipped whole sections, but every remark that he did make gave the work a new, interesting complexion, so that at the end of the rehearsal even indifferent musicians were carried away by enthusiasm.

Nikisch was not good at training orchestras; he was lacking in industry and patience. He was the born guest conductor, an improvisor of genius who had hardly his equal for the apparent ease and pleasing way in which he attained the greatest effects, of course simply through his complete mastery of his subject. It cannot be disputed that he was one of the greatest conductors, from whom we young people could learn an infinite deal.

Felix Mottl conducted among other operas *The Taming of the Shrew* of Götz and *Figaro*. At that time, after the brilliance and virtuosity of Nikisch, he disappointed us; now I can much better appreciate his natural musical gifts and warm feelings. In *Don Giovanni*, which closed the series of his guest performances, a double-bass for the stage music in the finale of the first act was suddenly found to be missing. At the last moment the orchestra manager rushed up to me, who was sitting as always in the orchestra pit with the score, and begged me to help them out. I was dragged into a dressing-room, got into a costume and make-up and ran on to the stage. Someone pushed a double-bass into my hand. A musician called to me, "Look out for your intonation; with a double-bass the intervals are a yard apart!" In spite of this I said I was willing to go on if I was to perform only in the orchestra that played the 3/8 section. Here the part for the double-bass consists almost entirely of the open G string and the D a fifth above it. To be certain of striking this note I carefully sought out the place where the D was to be pressed down, and marked it with a chalk line. Never afterwards, and probably never before, was this part played with greater neatness or more correct intonation!

At this time also the first performance of Richard Strauss's *Salome* took place. This work had roused us to such enthusiasm from reading the piano score that we could hardly wait to hear how it sounded on an orchestra. But this time we students were not called in as reinforcements. Attendance at the rehearsals was strictly forbidden, and the composer, who was present, or in his place his publisher, took the greatest care that to increase the effect of the surprise no outsider should hear any of the new music before the first night.

I could not wait all that time! Before the dress rehearsal began I went with Adolf and a few friends to the orchestra door in Richard Wagner Street and made a last attempt to get past the doorkeeper. But this, too, failed, and I climbed the wall of the opera house by the gutter, up to the third storey, where an open window led to the dressing-room of the chorus. From there I reached the auditorium without incident. Here, however, I felt so ill at ease among the few elegant guests that after a short time I preferred to sheer off and, taking the same route as before, landed in the street again, greeted by the shouts of my friends.

61

The sensation that Strauss produced on us was shortly afterwards diminished by the interest we took in another composer whom we got to know. This was Max Reger, whose *Sinfonietta*, shortly after the scandal it had caused in Munich, was given its first performance under Steinbach in the Gürzenich concerts. The *Sinfonietta* is such an overloaded work that it is difficult to hear the essential. One voice stifles another, and it is hardly possible for the ear to follow the continuous changes of harmony. In spite of this, Reger's first-born contains so much splendid music that we worked at it day and night. Later, Adolf learnt Reger's Violin Concerto by heart in a very short time, so that we were soon able to perform it to the Master.

From this time dated our relations with Max Reger—at first simply the deepest artistic respect, it developed in time into a personal friendship which lasted till his early death.

Gandhi, in his autobiography, tells of the bad influence an older friend had on him in his youth. What seemed to him sacred and worthy of veneration the other turned to ridicule; he led him astray to the pleasures of eating meat, smoking and other things. A similar effect was produced on me at that time by an older fellow-student in the conducting class. He was a very wealthy Dutchman, and had very little idea of the real nature of music. He could hardly play the piano at all, he played the violin wretchedly, and had only the slightest notion of the technical and theoretical principles of his profession. I should never have had anything to do with him if he had not had the talent of recognising and imitating in their smallest details the outward peculiarities of the celebrated conductors of the day. "Just how he cleared his throat and spat[1] . . ." successfully he'd spied out *that*.

My so-called friend had a great number of conducting sticks belonging to celebrated conductors, among them one that Nikisch had left behind. Using the corresponding stick, he

[1] Schiller: Wie er sich räuspert und wie er spuckt. (Wallenstein.)

showed me exactly how Mengelberg prepared the clash of the cymbals in the third movement of Tchaikowsky's *Pathetic*, how Weingartner indicated the trombone entry in the storm in the Pastoral Symphony with a thrust, and many other such absurdities. I used to stand in front of the looking-glass and, while practising with different types of baton, became the victim of a number of mannerisms which for a time seemed more important to me than the search for the inner content of a work of art and its interpretation. Thank goodness this aberration did not last long.

At last, in Steinbach's absence, the hour came when I was allowed to appear before the orchestra as a conductor. Professor Waldemar von Baussnern, who took his place, asked us students of conducting which of us knew Lalo's E Minor Violin Concerto. I was the only one who did. I got on to the rostrum, pulled out of my coat-sleeve the baton which, like a field-marshal, I always took with me (on this occasion Mottl's style) and began to conduct. A week later, at the next rehearsal, Steinbach had returned, and when Lalo's Concerto was called for and I announced that I was the conductor he was astonished and angry. He shouted out at me, "But you are not to conduct yet! Have done with your impertinence!"

However, my abashed, disappointed expression made him change his mind, so that he condescended to allow me to proceed. I shoved the desk to one side and conducted the first movement by heart. Then something unexpected took place. Steinbach came up to me, embraced me, and cried aloud, "This is the conductor of the future!" He could express his joyful emotion in no other way but by giving me ten marks—a gold piece—and told me "to have a good time".

I was congratulated on all sides, and went home in bliss. There Adolf, as leader of "my" orchestra, had already announced my success. At that time we were living in the centre of Cologne, in a little side street, through which the big vegetable trucks went in the early morning to market. During those times the traffic was lively. The next day, after a restless night,

I got up very early and found a considerable crowd of people collected in front of our house. Market women, peasants, street workers, were gaping at a gigantic placard which during the night had been fastened to the ground-floor windows of our house. On it one could read in huge letters: "In this house lives the conductor of the future!"

Some of my friends in the orchestra had treated themselves to this joke. But all this did not interfere with my happiness, especially as Steinbach the following day appointed me to conduct the Brahms D Major Serenade, at the next end-of-term concert. The evening came. In my movements I aimed at economy and elegance; consciously and unconsciously I imitated Weingartner. I mounted the rostrum and signed condescendingly to the platform attendant, under the eyes of the packed auditorium, that he was to remove the conductor's desk. This showed clearly that I intended to conduct the *Serenade* by heart—a custom which was then much more unusual than it is to-day, and which aroused the excitement on which I had reckoned. Adolf, the leader of the orchestra, whispered audibly, "Stupid ape!" which in no way disturbed me.

Steinbach this time was much more reserved than before; my vanity, my idiotic behaviour, must have been unsympathetic to him. He had, however, enough experience to pass over in silence such fleeting weaknesses, while my old friend Boettcher as well as Adolf on the way home never stopped their ironical remarks. I soon pulled myself together and very quickly realised that I was really too good for such airs and graces.

Adolf and I were the only ones chosen for the last public end-of-term concert of the conservatoire in the big Gürzenich hall. Adolf had prepared the Brahms Violin Concerto, for which I was to conduct the orchestral accompaniment. Besides that, he had composed a small orchestral work, the first performance of which I was to conduct. Finally, I was to play the Brahms D Minor Piano Concerto conducted by Steinbach himself.

Adolf and Fritz, aged 10 and 11

But all fell out differently. In one of the last rehearsals I had a serious conflict with Steinbach. He suddenly wished me to use a different technique in conducting—in fact, his own. He was of middle height, thick-set and corpulent; I was tall and unusually slim, so that I could not adopt Steinbach's method of reaching out his arm, or the flick of the right wrist in beating a bar in 3/4 time, which brought with it a circular movement of the baton.

At first modestly, then energetically, I defended myself against Steinbach's instructions, whereupon he forbade me to conduct in the concert on account of insubordination. I was only allowed to perform the first movement of the Brahms Piano Concerto. And it was in this way that the concert took place. Many people, who had known me only as accompanist, assistant repetiteur or performer of chamber music were astonished to find I was a soloist with a respectable technique. But I still felt, though I would not show it, the bitter disappointment of not having bade farewell to the conservatoire in my real profession of conducting.

I was "cross" with Steinbach. I attempted as soon as possible to break off all relations with the conservatoire, which had suddenly become distasteful to me. Among the visitors to the Festival was Kapellmeister H. H. W., who was on the point of taking up the post of first kapellmeister in the Deutsches Theater in Riga. I got into touch with him and signed a contract for a year for the winter season in that theatre, with a monthly salary of seventy-five Russian roubles, then about a hundred and fifty marks. This was not enough to live on, too much to die on, especially as my parents reckoned on me for further assistance. I had no idea what was in the contract, which my father had to sign with me as I was a minor. The mere words "The Deutsches Theater engages Herrn Kapellmeister Fritz Busch" had sufficed to decide me to accept.

It was June 1909, and my arrival at Riga at the end of August was fixed. My wardrobe was more than modest and savings with which to improve it were not at hand. This problem was recognised by the first double-bass of the town orchestra, an excellent, kind, elderly man. He offered to lend me the enormous sum of 500 marks with which I could, outwardly at any rate, do justice to the claims appropriate to the Kapellmeister of a theatre where Bruno Walter had formerly worked and, before him, Richard Wagner.

I had just closed with the Riga contract when the position of kapellmeister for the summer season in the health resort of Bad Pyrmont fell vacant. The final word in making the appointment was with the new manager of the health resort, a Herr von Beckerath, belonging to the well-known Rhineland family and son of an old friend of Johannes Brahms. It would surely be easy to make contact with him by using this composer's name if Steinbach would help—but I was "cross" with him!

He still knew nothing of my intention of going to Russia, and as I had to say good-bye to him I swallowed my feelings and made my request at the same time. A moving scene took place; his warm-hearted nature and affection for me showed themselves at once; all the vexation of past weeks was forgotten; he drew up a letter in his own handwriting and handed it over to me open. I read what the master thought in his heart of his young pupil, expressed in words which I have treasured all my life.

I at once journeyed to Bad Pyrmont dressed up, in spite of the heat, in a new immensely long frock-coat with a gaily-coloured waistcoat, a shiny green and red tie which did not cover the stud of the high, stiff-necked collar, a straw hat and—yellow shoes! Up to then I had not bothered myself about the demands of fashion. Herr Kurdirektor Beckerath, a very well-groomed and punctilious elderly gentleman, cast a fleeting glance at my appearance and then announced that he saw no possibilities for me. I begged him to allow me to conduct at least *one* concert and suggested a Beethoven-Brahms evening. "To carry out such a programme as it should be done," he said, in an experienced way, "you would need an orchestra of sixty musicians. Our orchestra numbers thirty-three and money to increase it is not available with my budget. Many thanks for your visit."

Standing in the street I was obliged to confess that our conversation had been short and quite unsuccessful. For a time I walked up and down to consider what further steps to take so as not to let the opportunity escape without a further struggle. Hastily I once more confronted the man to whom I wished to entrust my fate. I repeated my proposal of a Beethoven-Brahms evening but added that I myself would be responsible for the augmentation of the orchestra and would place at his disposal my brother as soloist in the Violin Concerto—also free of charge. Should the concert be a great financial success it would be left to him to make a contribution to the travelling expenses of the musicians from other districts. Surprisingly enough the bargain was struck.

I went back to Cologne by the next train and collected twenty-five to thirty of our friends and colleagues in one of the rooms of the conservatoire. I explained to them that I expected from their sense of decency that they would help me in the start of my career and that to begin with they would collaborate without pay in my symphony concert on my "appointment" at Pyrmont. In the first place they would themselves have to pay even for fourth-class railway tickets, while I would see to finding free hospitality for them—in short do my best to turn the undertaking into a pleasant summer outing. If I was successful, which none of those present could doubt for a moment, I should know how to repay their friendly services later on. They all agreed.

The next day I was back in Pyrmont. Boettcher, torn between enjoyment and scepticism, contemplated with interest the development of the enterprise. Meanwhile he procured a room for me in the comfortable house of his well-to-do sister who was settled in Pyrmont. The day after my arrival my first visit was to the owner and editor of the Pyrmont newspaper. I very soon won this man's favour and he placed his pages at

67

my disposal unconditionally—I believe he was actually delighted to have journalistic material for a fortnight without having to pay for it. Every day the astonished visitors to the baths were forced to realise, through a pitiless procession of criticism, analyses, biographical sketches and the like, that an unusual artistic experience awaited the quiet health resort.

The posters which I had had put up bore the names of the composers in small letters while that of the conductor stood out in big type. At night I went out through the streets with glue-pot and brush to stick up posters with my own hands wherever they seemed to me to be lacking—a method which the propaganda of political parties was later to adopt. I appeared at least twice every day in the shops that had undertaken advance booking to verify how the receipts were coming in. After a few days I could already reckon on success, for there was certain to be a full house. The princely court had graciously consented to be present.

The manager of the baths, who was now highly delighted, much amused and full of enthusiasm, once the performance was sold out placed at my disposal a sum of money which relieved me of all fears as to the payment of my Cologne friends. They appeared punctually at the final rehearsal; contact was immediately made with the local orchestra, consisting of the musicians from the small court and town theatres. The concert in D Major took place. Joachim's injunction to take into consideration the relation of the various keys in building a programme was at that time unknown to me.

My programme consisted of Weber's *Oberon* Overture, Beethoven's Violin Concerto, and the Second Symphony of Brahms. On this important evening I used the stick Nikisch had left behind. Still by no means free of eccentricities, I had arranged for the beginning of the coda in the Overture to throw both my arms suddenly in the air at the up beat of the gallant final theme. As if to punish me, the stick caught in the glass chandelier hanging over my head and snapped, at the same time breaking some of the prisms. A hail of splinters fell over me and success was assured! After that, the Violin Concerto and the Brahms Symphony—this time the desk was modestly removed during the interval—presented no problems.

The Prince and Princess sat in the front row in big red upholstered chairs with gilt arms. It was in the extraordinarily beautiful "White Room" which unfortunately very soon afterwards fell a victim to fire. The Prince was completely unmusical, the Princess hard of hearing. She loved music with all her heart, however, and was a charming woman. In the interval the royalties addressed me graciously, and the assembled audience listened from a respectful distance, but without the slightest difficulty, to my conversation with the deaf princess. I got the contract. For three years I was engaged for the summer months with a guaranteed salary of 500 marks a month—a sum unusually high for those days. Besides that, the "court kapellmeister" received the full takings of a benefit concert which, later, during the time of my Pyrmont activities, was commuted by the management to a fixed sum of 1,200 marks.

I was then nineteen years old and had still found time in the midst of my worries and struggles to fall deeply in love and become secretly engaged. As in an experience of Mark Twain's —or of Tamino's, who, however, had to learn to play the flute before becoming engaged—the sight of a photograph which Karl Boettcher showed me, had been enough to inspire me. It was the portrait of his niece, the only daughter of his brother, Dr. Friedrich Boettcher. After many years' activity as a writer —well known at the time—and member of the Reichstag for Waldeck and Pyrmont, he had recently returned from Berlin to his birthplace of Mengeringhausen. In this small idyllic country town, with its medieval timbered houses and crooked gothic church tower, on a visit to Karl Boettcher in the Easter holidays, I got to know my future wife.

The Boettchers were, as can easily be understood, at first horrified at our intentions. To make them more favourable to our future union was one of the objects of my Pyrmont concert

69

and of a second one which followed it. We brought our heavy guns to bear by putting together a programme consisting entirely of my future father-in-law's favourite pieces, and this already brought us nearer to our goal. The parents and daughter came to the Pyrmont concerts; they were all musical and my fiancée had been studying the violin for some years at the Berlin Hochschule; Joachim was to have taken her as a pupil when, to her abiding grief, he died.

With the Pyrmont contract in my pocket, I set off in August 1909 across the Baltic to Riga. A new chapter in my life was to begin.

Chapter Three

RIGA

Misery acquaints a man with strange bedfellows.

SHAKESPEARE

I N 1909 the town still belonged to Old Russia, but as regards culture the German element dominated. One can read about the Deutsches Theater, where I was engaged, in Richard Wagner's Autobiography. In spite of his lamentations the artistic performances of this establishment in the year 1838 must have been better than in 1909.

The director of the Deutsches Theater was a certain Dr. D. from Prague, a pronounced psychopath, who only felt in good health if he had succeeded in producing such a confusion on the stage, by dint of his intrigues, that everyone concerned was at his wits' end.

To obtain a box-office success it was the custom to perform operettas, and *The Merry Widow*, *The Divorced Wife*, *The Merry Peasant*, and such-like belonged to the standing repertory of the season 1909–10. Besides the first kapellmeister H.H.W., a second, Kapellmeister K., was to hand, a man completely destroyed by drink and entirely devoid of ideals. But even this colleague had lost the desire of perpetually conducting nothing but operettas, especially as the performances had become so careless that not a soul dared to think of even attempting an improvement. The conducting of these operettas was therefore handed over to me, without providing me with the slightest possibility of rehearsing. The result was what might have been expected, but nobody cared.

With my salary of 150 marks a month I was obliged to be extremely economical, especially as I had promised to send my family money regularly. So I took a room with the widow of a Pastor Green, a cheap room looking on to the court, in the

71

Albertska-Ulica, and very modestly furnished. It did however contain a big table on which I installed a gigantic inkstand and wrote industriously and in great detail to my—at that time—secret fiancée. A further ornament of this room was a grand piano which the firm of Ibach, well known in the Rhineland at that time, had placed freely at my disposal through their Russian representative. My exacting duties at the theatre unfortunately allowed little opportunity to employ the grand piano; I chiefly made use of the inkstand.

I had been some months away from home when, to my great astonishment, my parents suddenly announced an imminent visit from Adolf—a striking example of the Busch family feeling as well as of their carelessness in money matters. I fetched Adolf from the station and was horrified at his appearance as I embraced him on his arrival. When we parted he had been a slim, tall youth of about eighteen; what I now held in my arms was an enormous thick-set man from the sight of whom I could not turn my terrified eyes. Adolf whispered to me, "Be quiet; I'll explain everything later."

We took a cab, and as soon as we were out of reach of the Russian customs office he explained the cause of his corpulence; under his winter overcoat he was wearing a fur which our kind mother had given him for me so that I should not feel the cold Russian winter too severely. On arriving at my room on the court, in which a second bed in the shape of a sofa had been installed, Adolf freed himself of overcoat and fur, which latter could not compete with Russian furs. It was not a dignified sable, neither mink nor astrachan, but came from a lowly German sheep. He had brought coals to Newcastle. But the fur achieved its purpose to Mother's and my satisfaction.

Adolf was extremely anxious to know what opera he would be able to hear me conduct. I answered, "*The Juggler.*" His astounded face caused me to add that it was a "farce with songs". I could tell him nothing about its contents or its music, as I should only get to know the work shortly before the performance.

I must be spared a description of the evening, over which it is better to draw the veil of oblivion. I only know that after the overture and the rise of the curtain the chorus rushed excitedly on to the stage to sing, "No, we will no longer wait, We must see the magistrate!" In my "score"—a too euphemistic description of the bundle of manuscript music lying on my desk—there appeared an Allegro in 2/4 time. The chorus sang in the tempo of Robert Schumann: "As fast as possible"— "faster". The dialogue that followed was in full flow when I and my orchestra had reached the end. And so on.

We brothers went sadly home and even Adolf, once he had grasped the situation, felt that any criticism of my conducting would be ill-timed. No musician in the world could have done better. We went to bed and, as we had hardly spoken to each other before, Adolf began to hold forth.

It was already late at night when he reached Reger's latest chamber music compositions, still unknown to me. Not to disturb the other lodgers, Adolf wanted me, with my tired head, to take in the wild modulations which he sketched out for me somewhat as Johann Sebastian Bach, blind and dying, dictated the Choral "Wenn wir in höchsten Nöten sein" to his pupil Altnikol, who took it down with a quill pen. After the slavery of the previous day and the agitation of the performance of The Juggler, in which in the end the conductor himself had to juggle his way along, I was not capable of this mental exertion. I asked Adolf to play the relevant passages as softly as possible on the Ibach piano.

There was no electric light at hand, so that a candle had to serve for illumination. By its miserable light Adolf got out of bed to place himself at the piano barefooted and in his nightshirt. In the badly-lit, unknown room he stumbled, chairs and table flew in every direction, and to our indescribable horror we saw that the inkstand with the purple ink had fallen and emptied its contents over the keys of the piano Ibach had so generously placed at my disposal.

My whole future seemed to be annihilated. Never, I thought,

shall I be able to raise enough money to repair the damage. We could do nothing but creep silently and in lamentable mood back to bed. Hardly was the light out when Adolf asked timidly, "I say, is your bed as damp as mine?" In one leap I was out of bed and we then discovered that with our bare feet we had waded through the stream of ink on the floor. The bedclothes of the widow Green exhibited our footprints in glaring purple tints.

Once again the firm of Ibach showed their generosity, while the widow Green insisted on compensation for her bedclothes. Adolf, as a violinist, could reinforce a symphony concert under H.H.W. and in this way earn a few roubles with which the widow could be indemnified.

The programme of this concert was devoted to Brahms and contained, besides the Academic Festival Overture and the Fourth Symphony, the Piano Concerto in B Flat, for the solo part of which Artur Schnabel was engaged. In the general rehearsal the third horn was unexpectedly absent. A substitute could not be found. I had several times before taken part with the orchestra at the last moment, playing different instruments, and on this occasion was asked to undertake the part of the third horn. This was in accordance with my contract, by which I was bound "always to do anything that was required in the theatre as far as my musical powers permitted".

I took the horn and sat down in the orchestra. I did not play at all badly; Adolf had reason to be proud of his brother once more. I unfortunately thought it might be still better, and if I *had* to play the horn I ought to do it as well as possible. I therefore took the instrument home with me and began to play sustained notes, to practise scales and try out the ticklish passages in my part, until my lips, for long unaccustomed to this form of activity, swelled up and no longer brought forth any sound at all. I ought to have remembered Adolf's participation in my school orchestra.

Such a condition lasts for several days, during which one must avoid touching the mouthpiece. Nevertheless, they forced

74

me with threats to play, although I refused all responsibility.

The overture passed off without mischance. But in the piano concerto such frightful sounds emerged from my horn that Schnabel at the piano visibly shuddered. Adolf hung his head in shame and the conductor made despairing gestures to stop me. It served him right!

About twenty years later Artur Schnabel was playing as soloist in a concert at the Dresden Opera House under my direction. In a friendly conversation I asked him, who had travelled and seen so much, what was the worst musical experience he had ever had. After thinking for a moment he replied, "It was certainly at Riga, where a young horn player performed so appallingly that even to-day my breath fails me when I remember that evening."

By degrees my income had become in pressing need of improvement. Hans Schmidt, the music critic of the *Riga Rundschau*, which appeared in German, who was known as the poet of Brahms' *Sapphishe Ode*, engaged me as second critic. I tried to combine this with my fatiguing duties at the theatre.

In normal conditions and with goodwill on both sides, this twofold activity would have been quite possible. But my irritable director was boycotting this very *Riga Rundschau*. He had withdrawn free tickets from its critic after the stage setting of a play by Strindberg had been described—in my opinion justly—as "the work of an upholsterer". I therefore had to exercise my duties as critic secretly, as discovery would have led to instant dismissal.

Even Adolf—always ready for a dispute—advised me to hold on to the theatre at least till the moment when, as conductor, I should succeed in starting and finishing the chorus in *The Juggler* at the same time as the singers. Success here would help me to attain higher aims!

For a time all went well, until a mishap led to the discovery of my journalistic activities. I had to choose between the profession of critic and the profession of musician, however much it angered me that a very necessary source of my income should

75

dry up. In the theatre I quickly learned the necessary, though abominable, opera routine of conducting slovenly performances without rehearsals and to be proof against surprises, whether they came from the stage or the orchestra. But finally I was asked to take over the harp, an instrument I cannot bear anyway, at a performance of Gounod's *Faust*, from which the harpist was absent. At this I finally struck. A piano had been brought into the orchestra pit instead of the harp, and on this, instead of murmuring softly the delicate scale passages of the prelude, I thumped them out fortissimo in octaves which in strength were certainly not inferior to those of d'Albert in his period of "storm and stress".

A violent scene followed between the director, the Kapellmeister and myself and led to an unexpected development. Dr. D. would not have been the idiot who a few years later had to be shut up in an asylum if he had not suddenly completely changed his attitude towards me. He offered me the post of first kapellmeister for the following year and assigned to me for the coming weeks the production of an opera which I might select from among several. I decided on *Der Wildschütz* of Lortzing, and was able to have enough rehearsals to secure a good performance.

The agreement for the next year I very wisely left in suspense. I packed my things and travelled back to Germany, the richer for many experiences, if not always agreeable ones.

Chapter Four

AT BAD PYRMONT

A clever painter in Athens once allowed a connoisseur
to see a picture of Mars, and asked his opinion of it.
The connoisseur told him frankly that the picture did not
altogether please him. . . .
*   At that moment a young coxcomb entered and looked*
at the picture. "Oh!" he exclaimed at the first glance,
"Ye gods, what a masterpiece! . . ."
*   The painter was overcome with shame and looked*
sadly at the connoisseur. "Now," he said, "I am con-
vinced. You did me only too much honour."
*   The young coxcomb had hardly departed when the*
painter obliterated his War god.

CH. F. GELLERT

EVEN in Goethe's time Pyrmont was a much frequented
health resort, and Goethe himself—in the summer of 1801
—went there to recover from a severe illness. In spite of the
peculiar beauty of Pyrmont, which is surrounded by beech
woods, he could not refrain from ejaculating to Schiller,
"Every day it seems more and more tedious here."

I felt nothing of this tediousness when, a young musician,
full of curiosity and eager for action, I arrived at Pyrmont in
the spring of 1910. In this health resort, which was visited by
hardly any very sick people, the majority of those taking the
cure were young and not-so-young ladies. Music played a great
part in the cure, as did now and then the musicians themselves,
for they, with the actors of the charming little theatre, were the
chief representatives of the masculine sex. My predecessor, a
certain Kapellmeister H. who had retired from work at a great
age, must have been unsuitable in this connection, with his
voluminous red whiskers framing his good-natured face, and
his black frock coat and trousers, and necktie of the same

colour, which he apparently never took off. In the complaints book which the management had introduced and which offered the bored visitors opportunities of which they took full advantage to express their wishes and criticism, my predecessor came off badly. The disparaging comments reached their height in the following sentence: "This Kapellmeister H. has a large patch on the seat of his trousers which is most clearly visible when he conducts Richard Wagner's *Walküre*."

It was quite obviously advisable for the management to engage a young music director—especially as he had already abjured his straw hat and yellow shoes in favour of a dress-suit —to heighten the attractions of the concerts for the female sex, and the loss of these attractions caused by my early engagement produced a small wrinkle on Herr von Beckerath's brow which he could not conceal. Now he depended only on my musical powers.

My predecessor had not been destined from the cradle to the profession of conductor. His thick, cudgel-like conducting stick looked as if it had originated in the Pyrmont woods and had been carved out by the old man himself for his musical purposes. H. had been a flautist in some orchestra or other, and had achieved the position of kapellmeister on the grounds of reliability. My colleague had not mastered the art of reading a score. The whole well-arranged selection of works in the repertory comprised instead of scores an additional first violin part from which H. conducted. Beethoven's *Third Leonora Overture* was an exception; but this score I, on my side, could not use. When my predecessor, whose musical education was not profound, conducted this work, confused by the multiplicity of staves and in the effort not to lose control, he used to follow the first violin part with the forefinger of his left hand. He did this so vehemently that in the course of years big rents and spots had made their appearance and rendered it impossible for me to make use of the one and only score that was at hand.

Thus my first care was to secure as many scores as possible, even if they were only miniatures. Unexpected assistance came from the chief director of the Berlin publishing firm of Simrock who, chancing to be present in Pyrmont and being an enthusiastic member of my audience, gave me the complete orchestral works of Dvorak in score and parts. I now had what I wanted—plenty of splendid music, full of invention, in faultless condition. Without any previous rehearsals, for which there was no time, Dvorak's compositions were forthwith performed at first sight in the daily afternoon and evening concerts. Of course, in spite of this regular routine for Kapellmeister and orchestra, there were often mishaps; I therefore thought of a dodge. As soon as disaster threatened I gave a beat which arrested the course of the music; at the same time the drummer played a fortissimo roll, quickly becoming a diminuendo and allowing me to tell the orchestra softly but clearly at what point we could resume our daring performance.

I should like to deny here, as not corresponding to the facts, the assertion of an envious colleague that in my Pyrmont concerts hardly anything but drumrolls was to be heard!

Another catastrophe was countered with success. When the public would no longer do without its usual musical diet and the above-mentioned complaints book began to be full of grumbles, I received an injunction from the management to allow the name of Dvorak to disappear from the programmes and to replace it "in the main by pleasing music" such as the works of Paul Lincke.

This fertile constructor of operettas and revues, who had acquired in Berlin the greatest success with the public and a corresponding percentage of the takings, was quite peculiarly hated by Adolf and me. After brief consideration Adolf, who during the first weeks acted as leader of the orchestra I had collected, discovered a solution of genius to the problem. Correctly taking it for granted that our public had not very much perception as regards music, we inverted Schopenhauer's well-known sentence: "The important thing is not what one seems but what one actually is." We placed Paul Lincke's name

79

on the programme as "what seems" and played our Dvorak as "what actually is".

The catastrophe finally occurred when one afternoon, in the interval of the concert, the attendant brought me a visiting card: "Paul Lincke, Composer and Proprietor of the Apollo Publishing House, Berlin." I turned to Adolf for help. But he dodged me in the very moment when his brotherly support was most needed. I had to bear the consequences of our actions alone and went bravely to the terrace where Paul Lincke, a dissipated gentleman of exaggerated elegance, was already awaiting me. He at once invited me in friendly fashion to have some coffee, which I did not refuse. After that, however, he told me with decision that the fraud I had been carrying on with his name for some weeks must now stop.

"For a fortnight," he said, "I have been taking the cure at Pyrmont. In each of your programmes the name of one of my compositions appears. I have, however, so far not heard a single one, but always nothing but the works of Dvorak. I must ask you for an explanation."

The undertones of his voice could no longer be described as "friendly". In the end, he said he would be satisfied with the prospect of having his damaged reputation as a composer rehabilitated by several Paul Lincke evenings, which I offered to arrange for him in the Park, with red illuminations. In this way his music would really be heard.

I artfully persuaded the great man to undertake the conducting of these evenings personally. Adolf and I withdrew meanwhile to our lodgings and played sonatas by Bach and Beethoven. Everyone was satisfied.

After the departure of the popular composer I took care that some of his works should be performed in the morning concerts which I did not direct. I continued to conduct Dvorak's works, which few kapellmeisters nowadays can know as well as I do. But henceforth Dvorak's name was prudently replaced only by that of composers who already lay in the grave, so that their startling appearance at Pyrmont was not so likely to occur.

In spite of the rise in Dvorak's stock which I caused at that time at Pyrmont I naturally tried to avoid one-sidedness in music. I had to thank splendid renderings by Nikisch for the first stimulus towards busying myself with the symphonies of Schumann, which Steinbach obviously did not value very highly. I organised at Pyrmont a Schumann Festival, and included as well as the Fourth Symphony the seldom played *Fantasy for Violin and Orchestra* with Adolf as soloist, and the melodrama *Manfred*. For this, Ludwig Wüllner was invited. The choruses in *Manfred* were sung by the visitors to the baths who, in reply to my advertisement, had come forward in great numbers, full of enthusiasm at the interruption to their medically prescribed boredom, and who blindly transferred their enthusiasm to the conductor. The chorus was augmented by the local Men's Choral Society.

Wüllner arrived with his sister, Anna, who had undertaken the part of Astarte. Simply to see the brother and sister on the platform together was an unusual experience. They were both exceptionally tall, very much alike in the cut of their faces, all their features were somewhat larger than life but full of expression. Wüllner's eyes were impressive and penetrating. In North America he was called "the singer without a voice", and his vivacious face, the splendid diction with which he managed the text and his great creative power, soon made one forget the poverty of his vocal material. He was a very fine musician and a great actor in the best tradition. I was bound to value his judgment. I was therefore disappointed that after the performance of the *Manfred* overture in the orchestral rehearsal his expressive face showed no recognition. Except for an appreciative smile at the *Chorus of Mountain Spirits* which the visitors sang with a racy swing, he remained during the rest of the rehearsal without giving any sign of approval.

Somewhat intimidated, I asked him on the way home straight out how he had liked my conducting, and received this answer: "Young man, you are doubtless gifted but you have not the slightest idea what lies behind the notes of this

81

magnificent composition. The spirit, the true beauty of this music is a completely dead letter to you, and I am afraid that you will never grasp it, as you are much too conceited."

After an uncomfortable silence in which the memory of how my ladies' chorus had deified me flashed swiftly and painfully through my mind, I asked Wüllner with a red face if he would give me the grounds of his criticism more definitely.

He said he considered such an undertaking to be hopeless. His explanation of the style of *Manfred* alone would take up hours of time, and for such an exertion he might have time and strength but I probably should not.

That same afternoon we met in my room where Wüllner, at the piano, gave me a notion of the spirit of Schumann's music. I began to realise that romantic music, and especially Schumann's, could not do without a certain freedom of expression. Later, as a result of this insight, I also reached the conviction that Schumann's instrumental works demand a quite peculiar feeling for sound on the part of the conductor and that thus, to bring the listener closer to its complete beauty, he must not shrink from such radical touching up as both Mahler and Weingartner employed.

These hours with Wüllner confirmed me in the opinion which, though not new to me, had nevertheless up to now been kept back by a naïve, youthful delight in my own powers—the opinion that the greatest technical perfection can only be a foundation—art only begins with what one can discover and express "behind the notes".

I have never forgotten Wüllner and what I owe him as a musician. It was with great pleasure that I repeated the performance of *Manfred* with him at different stages of my professional life—at Aix, Stuttgart, Dresden. At the latter place I was in the prime of life and he had become very old. He again brought his sister with him as Astarte. They were now both snow white, but the power of expression in their faces had not suffered. After the performance, which Wüllner described as one of the most beautiful in all his life, I ventured to reply:

"So what you once said to me at Pyrmont was after all not in vain."

He had quite forgotten that he had once put a young kapellmeister on the right path by straightforward if unsparing criticism, and he felt embarrassed when, after the last performance of *Manfred* which we gave together, the Dresden Generalmusikdirektor gave him hearty thanks for it.

In my capacity of court Kapellmeister it fell to me besides my summer duties to prepare in the course of the winter two court concerts in the royal castle of Arolsen, at which I played the piano. This suited me very well as Arolsen was only half an hour distant from Mengeringhausen. In the same country hotel which I frequented, Weingartner, exactly thirty years before, had lodged for exactly the same reason, namely, a pretty girl.

The court concerts were a headache for me. Their Royal Highnesses wanted the most considerable artists in Germany to perform at them. Conditions: second-class return ticket and free board and lodging at the best hotel in the town. (There were two.) Fee?

The Court Chamberlain, with his feudal aspect, did not understand. "Fee? But it is an honour for the artists to be allowed to perform before Their Royal Highnesses. Of course no fee will be paid."

"Very well," I said. "How about a decoration?"

"Decoration? I don't understand you. If the artists please" (these were the very words of Freiherr von H.) "then in the following year they will *perhaps* be invited a second time. If they then please again they will *perhaps* be honoured by a decoration."

I had not much hope of achieving anything worth while on this basis, and subsequently was surprised at how many first-rate artists nevertheless accepted invitations even to the most inferior German courts in the hope of "*perhaps*" some day receiving a decoration.

Max Reger, whom I once invited amongst others in the following years to play his Beethoven Variations with me on

83

two pianos, was an exception. It is true he did not decline the invitation but he demanded his distinction without delay. He wished to know whether it would be the *gold* medal for art and science? Whether it would be the *large* gold medal? Whether it would be the large gold medal with the red ribbon?

I had not reckoned with this knowledge of the German system of decorations, which was in no way inferior to his masterly command of the most intricate contrapuntal art. Letter followed letter until I could guarantee everything he wished for.

On a cold day in January he arrived early in the morning, getting out sleepily from his compartment, at the small station lying a short distance from the small town of Arolsen. He was an extraordinarily tall man with tiny feet and an ugly child-like face over which in winter a beaver-skin cap throned it. We went to the castle to rehearse and the Princess immediately made her appearance, a still young, attractive woman with a real understanding of music. Perhaps it was innate in her from her Bohemian origin, of which I was also reminded by her dark, rather harsh-featured face. In any case she seemed somewhat isolated from the jovial, pleasure-loving Prince. Her deafness, which she had tried gracefully to master, made her shy and to some extent repressed her natural, cordial disposition.

I had drawn Reger's attention to the fact that he must speak very loudly to her. In an interval after I had presented Reger, she asked in the course of the conversation: "Professor, why do you play on an Ibach piano and not on a Steinway?" Reger bellowed through the room: "You know, Your Highness, they pay much more!"[1] Princess Bathildis showed complete understanding for this point of view.

I had less understanding for Reger's weakness for decorations. I was irritated and became more so when he began to worry me—he must have his Order at once—with the somewhat threadbare argument that the Prince would take it ill if he was not wearing it at the court concert!

[1] Wissen's, Hoheit, die zahlen vüll mehr!

84

I had to run to the Chamberlain again, who finally handed out the Order. But even then the farce was not at an end; Reger declared, with complete seriousness, that the chambermaid was not capable of sewing the medal of the Order correctly on to the ribbon from which it hung and that my fiancée must come to undertake the business. I telephoned, she came, and accomplished the sewing to Reger's complete satisfaction.

Unfortunately the Master, newly adorned in his gold medal, now came in sight of the two artists who were taking part in the concert—a lady violinist, and a lady singer who was familiar with Reger's works. It must be said that he did nothing to spare them the sight but, on the contrary, rather threw out his chest like a peacock in front of them. For nothing in the world would he have missed the fun of thus challenging their vanity and envy, and was heartily delighted when they swallowed the bait. Their cries of: "And I . . . ?" "But I . . . ?" put him in the best humour.

Of course I had not omitted to ask Reger why he was so mad for orders and titles; but we could never come to an agreement on this point. Reger, who in his intercourse with highly-placed personages had himself a refreshing naturalness which he made full use of during his years at Meiningen, could not bear the court toadies. In this he was right, as a general rule. The freer and more natural the princes showed themselves the stiffer and more arrogant were their entourage in general, and the smaller the court the more ceremonious the etiquette. Reger became angry when, as he expressed himself in the Bavarian dialect, "swollen-headed"[1] aristocrats looked down on him on account of his lowly descent. It pleased him if he could out-trump them with decorations. To this day, when no one can reproach me with youth and ignorance of life as Reger then did, I have not learnt to understand this form of pleasure.

After the excellent Berlin Blüthner Orchestra had been engaged for Pyrmont at my suggestion for the season 1911,

[1] Grosskopfete.

85

I at once invited Max Reger to conduct some of his works there at a music festival which lasted several days.

My passionate interest in Reger's works had never abated since I had accompanied Adolf on the piano in a performance of the violin concerto at the Cologne conservatoire. The *Hiller Variations* Op. 100 had already been written, a work that contains more genuine music and masterly skill than all the designs on music paper, as Bülow once called them, that have been made from Brahms to now. Reger conducted it at that time at Pyrmont.

Immediately on the arrival of my fiancée, who had come to this music festival with her parents, I told her very seriously that after the general rehearsal she must tell me truthfully whether she liked this music or not. In the latter case, there could be no thought of marriage!

As I have already said, my fiancée had studied music, played a great deal of chamber music, and was sufficiently well up in orchestral literature to give a judgment based on musical understanding. She was also truthful; often more so than I liked.

After the general rehearsal of the *Hiller Variations* we agreed that we could carry on with the marriage. The ceremony took place in August 1911 on Goethe's birthday in the old Mengeringhausen church.

Always suspicious where a musical performance I knew nothing about was concerned, I tried the venerable church organ a few days beforehand. I was not much disturbed by the fact that it was more than a tone too low, as not I, but the schoolmaster, Zick, had to play it. But it possessed a stop on which stood in faded letters the words *Bass Trombone*. When one pulled out this stop the organ creaked, crashed and rattled so that it was impossible not to laugh. I begged Zick on no account to use this stop and he promised me he would not.

The solemn moment of exchanging rings arrived; the numerous congregation, after a short prelude on the organ, sang "Now Thank We All our God". Then was heard a frightful growl. The noise made it impossible for me to remain

86

serious, but remembering the situation I bit my lips and only whispered angrily to my bride: "After all, Zick *has* pulled out the trombone stop!"

"Sh!" she said, "it is only Ohlendorf, the doctor, singing."

My two court concerts in the winter and the summer season at Pyrmont had not provided enough to marry on. I had therefore applied for the vacant post of conductor to the Gotha Musical Society. From amongst almost two hundred candidates I was chosen, originally, as I later discovered, on the grounds of my—handwriting; on the same principle as I was in the habit of selecting the members of my orchestra. Nevertheless, before finally giving me the appointment they wished to see me personally. I obtained a short leave of absence from Pyrmont and appeared before the notabilities of the town of Gotha; they were collected round a large beer table in the summer garden of the inn, to inspect the applicant.

When I came forward, a paralysed silence fell upon them and I realised that they had expected more from the personal appearance of the newcomer. Only twenty-one years old, thin and tall, I certainly looked so youthful that a refusal would have been easy to understand. But in spite of this I obtained the post, which helped me to a wife and a very good mixed chorus. During the winter of 1911–12 I conducted the *Creation* of Haydn and other choral works partly with the co-operation of the Meiningen court orchestra, which Reger let me have. He had shortly before become the successor of Wilhelm Berger in Meiningen, which was not far from Gotha, and often made life difficult for me by exhibiting his insatiable love of playing— for instance when, as court Kapellmeister, he snatched from me a chamber music concert at Hildburghausen and at the same time deprived me of a fee of fifty marks which would have been very welcome to my scanty household finances.

I went to Cassel as a substitute, to accompany a Belgian singer in a Lieder Recital. This, it is true, brought in twice that fee of Reger's, but also made me the laughing-stock of my father-in-law, who was in the audience. I had often refused, shuddering, to accompany the old gentleman in the Italian popular arias in which he sometimes revelled with his pretty tenor voice. His delight can be understood when the Belgian chose to add to his programme one after the other of these same trashy affairs which I was obliged to accompany, furious but helpless.

I had more enjoyment than on this evening in accompanying many good soloists who were engaged at Gotha, especially in my first meeting with Julia Culp, the excellent Lieder singer. Later in our friendship, which lasted for many years, we often laughed over the fact that Julia, who had arrived at Gotha with a remarkably modest programme, suddenly stopped singing in the middle of the rehearsal and called out: "But you play really *well*! Why didn't I know that before? I could have made quite a different programme!"

Owing to the limited means of the Gotha Music Society we could not give orchestral concerts regularly. I had better possibilities in sight, was receiving various offers, and had really arranged for a performance when the post of musical director at Aix-la-Chapelle unexpectedly became vacant. The celebrated town of Aix, with a musical atmosphere like that of Cologne where I had grown up, formed with Cologne and Düsseldorf the triple alliance of Rhineland towns in which, since the beginning of the nineteenth century, the yearly Lower Rhine music festival took place. For many years they had formed an organisation of great musical importance, and until the war of 1914 had hardly lost their former glory. Outstanding musicians of the nineteenth century, Mendelssohn, the Schumanns, Brahms, Joachim and many others rejoiced year in and year out in returning to the Lower Rhine Music Festivals.

My resolution to conquer Aix at any cost was immediately fixed. I encountered great scepticism as regards this venture from my mother-in-law, who had lived there as a child. She was passionately devoted to music, played the piano well and had been the pupil of the music director at Aix; she could only imagine him as a man of gravity and mature years. That a

88

youngster like her son-in-law should be accepted for this post appeared to her, for all her faith in my future, quite out of the question.

When my wife's parents had eventually heard about our secret engagement we could not take it ill that they were not very enthusiastic about it. I was at that time a nineteen-year-old pupil of the conservatoire who had not even passed the final examination. For that reason we had preferred to protect ourselves by preparing the way in letters, when Boettcher had his niece with him during the Opera Festival at Cologne. When she reached home her impulsive mother, sighing with vexation, received her with the words, "So now you have gone *completely* mad!" When her prudent daughter asked, "What does Father say?" her mother had to admit that he had said, "It's not quite the worst thing that could have happened."

It is easy to understand, nevertheless, that I felt it was important to prove to my wife's parents that on the contrary our union was actually the best thing that could have happened to their daughter.

For this reason, too, I had set my heart on winning the Aix post, in spite of all impediments. They were especially aggravated by the fact that I was a Protestant. In Aix, a severely Catholic city, this played an important part. Good luck smiled upon me in a surprising form. The manager of the baths at Aix, who had occasionally heard me at Pyrmont, selected me as his candidate. At the first glance he reminded one in a startling fashion of the Junker of Emperor Wilhelm's time who was represented in the comic papers with his turned-up waxed moustaches and resounding commando voice. Rittmeister d. R. Hey'l was nevertheless much more than this—a man capable of great enthusiasm and of untiring energy with which he supported my candidature in the proper quarters.

In a state of great nervous tension my wife and I made the journey to the old imperial city, the Palatinate of Charlemagne, which though so near to Cologne was still unknown to us. If we had stage-fright on this journey it was not on account of the music nor even of the appointment, but because I was faced with an experience I had never had before—I was to give an address to the Aix chorus. I remember that my wife and I wrote it in the train and that I learnt it by heart. My wife could not bring herself to listen to it, and only after the deed was done squeezed secretly into the concert hall. I conducted Mendelssohn's *Walpurgisnacht* and a Beethoven Symphony, and the following day got the place, perhaps from lack of a suitable Catholic of mature years. I said good-bye to Pyrmont and Gotha.

If I avoid as far as possible speaking of inner and outer struggles and deliberately emphasise the light side of a life full of varied experiences, it in no way means that I was spared the dark side of existence. Hans Sachs answers the question of Stolzing the Junker what a *Master* is: "Children, business, quarrels, strife—he who succeeds in singing a true song even then, he is called a Master."

Chapter Five

AIX-LA-CHAPELLE

If you only catch hold of the edge of the
Muse's garment you have done but little.

GOETHE

THE town looked important and had many visible links with
the past. The influence of the Netherlands was strong.
This impression was not confined to externals. The inhabitants,
too, immediately on the Belgian and Dutch frontiers, had
nothing of a typically German nature about them, to say nothing of Prussian stiffness. You heard them speak of Berlin not
without some pride, but as if it were the Far East.

In Aix there were many connections both of blood and business with the adjacent countries, especially Belgium. French
was much spoken. In many branches of industry Belgian
workmen were employed who went to and fro over the
frontier, morning and evening, and were unsurpassed at certain
crafts. In Aix it was possible, in the years before the war, to
imagine that all men were brothers, though it was just here that
this idea was to be destroyed for countless years.

This town possessed a great musical tradition. It had a good
orchestra, but the outstanding musical body was the Town
Choral Society of which, with its mixed chorus of trained
amateurs of about 250 members, Aix was justly proud.
Especially in unaccompanied singing, its performance was unsurpassed. Secretly, I could not contradict the music critic of
an Aix newspaper who, before my arrival at the above-mentioned concert to which I had come as a guest conductor, had
made the following sceptical remark in his column: "In the
future the Aix Choir is to be entrusted to very young hands. If
they fail in their promise, this precious instrument—one of the
most precious in Germany—nay, in the world—will be a thing

of the past!" The writer did not know how near the mark he was.

I had been brought up as an instrumentalist and as such had at first little interest in singing and in particular no liking for the sound of women's voices. Bach's Motets, Cantatas and Passion music I thought of as sung only by boys.

Once, years before, when Adolf sat down at the piano to sing and play to me by heart Schubert's *Schöne Müllerin*, my astonishment knew no bounds. I said nothing to him but instead of that went to our mother and said, "Look out for Adolf! He sings. He is in love." And so he was. This slight indication is enough to show what caused my insensitiveness to song in my early youth. I took it simply for an expression of feeling, which had very little to do with art.

Another thing was guilty of alienating me from singing and that was the amateurishness so common in the Rhineland, which led the typical slightly tipsy citizen to clap me gaily on the shoulder at festivities and ask if I could accompany him by heart in "Es liegt eine Krone im tiefen Rhein".[1] I knew it, and used to begin in a key too high for his voice. After the first verse I would modulate unobtrusively into a higher key so that the second verse began a full third too high. If my victim had enough strength or courage to get over this operation, on arriving at the third verse, which was a fourth higher, he was obliged to give up the business as hopeless.

Finally, I must state that in the narrow world of my childhood it is true that every imaginable musical instrument dangled on the walls of my father's little shop or stood or lay around, but there were no voices which were pleasant to listen to. In Westphalia—not far from the Rhineland, where song is, as it were, at home—the people are grave and reserved. So is the sound produced by their choral societies which nevertheless are to be found everywhere. Directly they made their appearance we young ones used to take flight.

After having received these impressions in my youth it re-

[1] A crown lies deep within the Rhine.

quired experience before I learnt to acknowledge that song is after all a valid art process. It is true that I had already acquired a certain insight as a choral conductor. But with the choirs with which I had had to do so far, the chief stress had always been on the musical qualities, not on the vocal qualities. All those Central German voices, although the singers understood easily and co-operated vivaciously, suffered from a certain poverty of tone. I had first of all to learn to recognise pure vocal beauty.

Aix converted the Saul into a Paul. At the beginning of my engagement the chorus sang Mozart's *Ave Verum* which they had studied with my predecessor, an adept at vocal music. The impression I received from it was a real experience.

To do justice to the demands which were now made upon me I had to engage in an intensive study of singing and the handling of voices. During the fifteen years in which I later conducted the Stuttgart and Dresden Opera and also the opera in many foreign theatres it was a satisfaction to find that my trouble had been rewarded. If I may boast of having given Aix a present in return I think I may say that I was fortunate enough to be able to unite musical life and feeling to the beautiful tone, the cultivation of which had been my predecessor's chief function. When I left Aix my chorus and I were, I believe, under equal obligation to each other.

How happy Germany was in the years before the war! As a town official appointed for life with a salary corresponding to that of a high state official—say, a *Landrat*,[1] and entitled to claim an ample pension on retiring, I was, at twenty-two, above any material cares. I cannot affirm that in later years this was always the case.

The mayor was a rich industrialist, enthusiastic for the arts, who often played in the orchestra on his Stradivarius violin. (The instrument was emphatically more valuable than the performance.) After a few weeks of my work he informed me that he felt it was his duty to raise my salary by no inconsiderable an amount.

[1] Chief administrative official in a rural district.

93

The Musikdirektor and his wife were looking for a suitable place to live in. To begin with, a promising house was refused to the Protestant because it was situated in a purely Catholic neighbourhood near the church of St. Mary. Then we were offered a beautiful aristocratic house at an astonishingly favourable rent. The fact that it was haunted did not matter to us much, especially as we succeeded by a piece of luck in getting on the track of the ghosts; in fact, this splendid property had been depreciated for many people by the phenomenon of a singular echo. To the heirs, the property seemed to be peculiarly suitable for the Musikdirektor because, besides innumerable large rooms and a spacious old garden, it possessed a hall, thirty-three feet long, which had served as a ballroom for many generations of marriageable Aix girls. We now installed two concert grand pianos, and with the help of a handsome carpet the problem of furnishing was solved in essentials —for the walls consisted of gigantic windows and mirrors. A few cupboards which stood between them took my music library, already at that time fairly large.

In those days a housewife had no particular difficulties with the servant problem such as are universal now. For instance, in the first years we had the girl we called "Dutch Marie", a real demon for cleaning, whose speciality was her original use of the German language. Translating from the Dutch, she said to my wife one evening when I rang at the front door: "The Herr Direktor is barking[1] downstairs."

"But, Marie, dogs bark," said my wife.

"Dogs, they yelp,"[2] persisted Marie obstinately.

The orchestra attendant, already advanced in years, tall, lanky and not averse from taking a drop—a fact to which the end of his nose bore witness—was called Holzbauer and was well known in the town, largely because he wore uniform—black trousers and a long blue jacket with shiny metal buttons. As "maid-of-all-work" he helped out when necessary with

[1] bellt.
[2] Honde, de blaffe.

94

endless good humour. His first duty with us was to sit on the box of a hired carriage beside the driver and go calling with the young married pair on the notables of the town.. Though I might have been his grandson, he respected my official position and never spoke to me except in a special way to indicate the distance between us. For him I was always HE.

"Yes, says HE. But HE hears nowt,"[1] he remarked to my wife, shaking his head. HE and Holzbauer remained to the end the best of friends.

The concert hall in the Kurhaus in Comphausbadstrasse could, it is true, accommodate only a thousand people, but its acoustics were ideal. It had a big organ and an extensive platform that had room for the necessary number of participants in such works as Mahler's Eighth Symphony or Pierné's *Children's Crusade* with its demands on an immense chorus.

The popular concerts on Saturday evening, with an admission fee of thirty-five pfennigs, were so much sought after that, besides the orchestra, hundreds of people occupied the platform. At my first popular concert I was bewildered by the unexpected sight of a crowd of listeners who were also spectators and gazed at me while I was at work in such a way that I found it difficult to bring my *Freischütz* Overture to a conclusion.

This hall, to-day lying in ashes, was once the scene of splendid concerts. As the town was rich, the best artists were invited to take part in them, and I was able to form musical and personal connections with them. Musical Societies with wealthy members permitted the institution of regular popular concerts, and of chamber music to which I invited the most splendid *ensembles*, amongst others the Rosé and Bohemian quartets, and I often played the piano with them.

It was most fortunate for me, a young man in his early twenties, that I was able to secure the performance of such great choral works as Bach's *St. Matthew* and *St. John Passion*, Beethoven's *Missa Solemnis*, Handel's *Messiah*, the *German*

---

[1] Dabei hört ER jarnich.

Requiem and *Alto Rhapsody* of Brahms, works by Reger and other contemporary composers.

In January 1913 I made the acquaintance of a musician who until his death was to play an important part in my life. This was Donald Francis Tovey, who had got to know Adolf on his first visit to London. Adolf's account of him was so enthusiastic that I invited him to Aix to play his piano concerto. Tovey at that time was in his middle thirties.

From the first, his uncanny memory astonished me. It is not too much to say that he knew the whole of music from Palestrina to Brahms thoroughly and completely and much of it by heart. For instance, if one sang him the second violin part of a rarely played Haydn quartet, a few bars were enough for him to name the place they came from and to drop some trenchant remarks on the peculiarities of the work. As a child he had been in touch with Joseph Joachim, who had immediately recognised his unusual gifts and, in a letter to Brahms, wrote how much he wished to bring him the little Donald.

Tovey was an excellent pianist and had also published a great deal of chamber music which, however, apart from a few exceptions, in spite of their deep learning lacked any great originality and in consequence did not do much towards the progress of art. Many of Tovey's English friends thought he knew too much to be a good composer. Richard Strauss had a somewhat similar opinion of Max Reger, but in Tovey's case there was more justification for the remark.

One symphony, which he completed in our house in the winter of 1913–14, was performed at Aix and was also accepted by Steinbach for a Gürzenich concert, but in consequence of the outbreak of war it was not performed there. An amusing incident, characteristic of my friend Donald, is connected with the first performance of this work at Aix. As the last movement of the symphony had not been completed when he arrived at Aix there was a hitch at the last moment in the copying of the parts. He had to finish some of this himself, in which I helped him, and we sat at this work till the morning of the

A wedding portrait, 1911

general rehearsal dawned. As we were on our way to it, worn out by our sleepless night, it happened that all the papers we had just written and which Tovey was carrying under his arm in an untidy bundle, slipped from him in the streaming rain into the muddy street. Both of us nearly howled. We hastily snatched up the scattered parts and I rushed with them to the librarian of the orchestra. He crossed himself and then seized a large sponge. The rehearsal began half an hour late. I am a fanatic for punctuality and exhorted Tovey somewhat crossly to say a few words of excuse to the musicians who were waiting impatiently. The way in which he did this was at the same time awkward and irresistible. He mounted the rostrum, related what had happened, thus losing considerably more time, and ended with the words:

"Gentlemen, you can think what you like of this music, but one thing you must admit. It is a symphony that has washed itself!"[1]

Tovey's appearance was remarkable. Of unusual height, with aristocratic features, he would have been a handsome man had it not been that his stooping figure, his clumsy movements and the savage neglect of his clothes, always of the best English material, made him into a grotesque figure. Like Reger, he had a special technique of dressing and undressing. It was his habit, without heeding the money and other things that fell out of his pockets, to strip off his clothes and let them lie on the floor so that in the morning he had only to slip back into them. Owing to his singular appearance he seemed older than he was; but on the other hand, when he was really old and his health had been ruined by illness, the merry, boyish laughter with which he accompanied his numerous tales, made him seem young. The unworldly, touching simplicity of his innocent heart was such that in Aix in 1914, on the evening we expected the birth of our first child, we were obliged to draw his atten-

[1] "Meine Herren, Sie können nun von diese Musik denken, was sie uollen, aber eins müssen sie zugeben: es ist ein Sinfonie die sich geuaschen hat!" [Gut gewaschen = a great success.]

tion to the expected happy event. His head being continually full of his own thoughts, what we were awaiting had entirely escaped him. But afterwards he showed the tenderest and warmest sympathy over our son, who became his godson.

Tovey spoke excellent German, using an uncommonly rich vocabulary, though he spoke with hesitation and ponderously because he was always searching for the best possible expression. In later years he was the only person who succeeded in explaining Einstein's theory of relativity to my wife and me so clearly that we retained an idea of its meaning for the space of three hours.

It would not be difficult for me to write a book about Tovey, the man and the artist, that would contain much worth knowing and of interest to musicians both young and mature. His compatriots, over whose want of understanding he used to complain in his youth, learnt in his later years to appreciate Tovey's value, which was shown in his numerous essays and contributions to the *Encyclopædia Britannica*. He was appointed professor of musical history to the University of Edinburgh, a position associated with the practical side of music, and a few years before his death in 1940 was knighted.

The natural elevation of his mind and his highly cultivated intellect threw everyone who came near him into the shade. In spite of his somewhat peculiar appearance Tovey never entered a circle of people whom he did not dominate in a very short time. His only rival was in himself—the sheer sincerity of his character rivalled his intellect. It was true of him that "the lower nature which masters us all" was in him non-existent.

When one thinks that in Aix, before the war, there were less than a hundred and fifty thousand inhabitants and that in the more than thirty big towns of Germany and also in countless smaller places—especially where there were courts—a similar love of music reigned, even if it was not so highly endowed as here described, one can imagine the degree of musical cultivation in the old *Reich*. But the glory was not to last long. My second season in Aix was hardly ended when war broke out.

General mobilisation followed in a few days after I had returned from a short stay in England in July 1914.

It struck me as curious that at about the same time as the beginning of the war the city of Cologne asked me to conduct two Gürzenich concerts and also suggested I should apply for the post of musical director and head of the conservatoire where I had been a pupil five years before. The post was vacant owing to Steinbach's departure. Shortly after the Lower Rhineland musical festival which began in Cologne in 1913, at which Steinbach made his last brilliant public appearance, the celebrated man fell a victim to an unjustifiable intrigue; he was obliged to resign, and did not long survive this blow.

I was sad at heart when I thought what changes had occurred in this short space of time and inwardly it went against the grain to seize Steinbach's place.

The war which broke out in August put an end to all further plans and projects. I became a soldier.

Chapter Six

WAR

War seems sweet to him that knows it not; but
he that knows it sorely feareth its approach.

PINDAR

As a musician I was hardly interested in political events up
to 1914. We lived quietly and happily in an orderly and
sober country which appeared to provide all men of goodwill
with work and food. The social upheavals that existed in spite
of this were not obvious to a carefree young man like me who
was occupied with music all day long. It is said that the period
between 1872 and 1914 which later appeared so enviable and
so normal was by no means normal, but was, on the contrary,
exceptional—the longest interval between wars in the last
century of German history. When this tranquillity was disturbed after forty years, only a relatively small number of
thoughtful people who had studied the background of world
history knew that it was by no means altruistic reasons that
formed the mainspring of the events which were beginning, as
war propaganda would have had us believe, but quite different,
matter-of-fact, materialistic considerations. This was as true in
Germany as in all the other countries that took part in the war.

To the small group of persons who knew what the game was
I certainly did not belong. I was twenty-four years old, had
lived almost exclusively for my profession and was grateful to
Germany for everything that made up my happiness—education, stimulus, a rapid career, an assured, even brilliant position,
work in plenty and the hope of a similar happy future for my
son. I should have thought myself very shabby if I had not paid
back to my country the benefits I had received from her, and
had not stood by her in the hour of danger. For this reason I
could not accept the opportunities that were repeatedly offered

me of working at music at home or behind the lines and to be relieved of service at the front. On the contrary, I immediately presented myself as a volunteer in Aix.

It was only on the field of battle that I began to wonder whether everything we had been told was true, but there I began to think it over quickly enough.

A bandsman who had played in my concerts and knew more about a soldier's life than I did, took me to the officer on duty in the barracks with all the pride which his unexpected superiority gave him.

At one end of the barracks yard stood a hundred young volunteers: workmen, students, tradespeople, collected in silence round a wagon on which an old white-haired colonel with a dashing moustache and a pair of restless eyes was making a violent speech. My bandsman pushed himself and me through the crowd to present the town Musikdirektor to the officer in a suitable manner. The Colonel, with a few friendly words, reached down his hand to me from the wagon and then suddenly called out in cutting tones: "You see that tree over there, about a hundred yards away? Go over there, and take up your position with your back to me. Wait for further orders."

I obeyed. I had often heard that in the army every order from a superior must be carried out even if one occasionally thought it unreasonable. So I stood obediently by my tree for about half an hour while the sun slowly set. I was then obliged to recognise that either the colonel who had given me the order was mad, or that I was for obeying it.

I went home undisturbed and early next morning tried my luck at getting taken into the German army a second time. At the door of the barracks I met an ambulance. As I afterwards discovered, it was taking the colonel to a lunatic asylum. The events of the last few days had finally upset the balance of his mind, which was already disturbed. With this extraordinary episode my war-time experiences began.

After a few weeks of infantry training, my regiment, which consisted entirely of volunteers, went first to Cologne, and in

September was moved to the depot at Ohrdruf in Thuringia, a little town which was well known to me.

In the winter of 1911–12, when I was working at Gotha, I had been approached by the proprietor of the Knippenberg Patent Mattress Factory. He was a man who was fond of singing and whose zeal in creating a mixed choir in his little town had been crowned with success. Herr Knippenberg was prepared to pay, out of his by no means meagre substance, for the additional singers necessary for the performance of an oratorio in Ohrdruf, in the secret hope that he would be given the part of baritone solo. At the first rehearsal I found in the inn a piano and five or six elderly ladies sitting round a table. In front of them was a coffee pot, and their hands were busily engaged in uninterrupted knitting. Three gentlemen, among them Herr Knippenberg, constituted the male choir. My fee corresponded to the numerical strength of this company.

With the co-operation of my Gotha choir, Schumann's *Paradise and the Peri* was actually performed, the nine or ten active members of the Ohrdruf musical society taking part with the hundred and fifty singers from Gotha! This performance had made me popular in Ohrdruf and its neighbourhood, and this now stood me in good stead. When the regiment entered the town my companions were not a little astonished to find the members of my former choir assembled at the entrance of the little town. They hailed me with tears in their eyes, shook hands with the valiant warrior, and slipped into his hands many parcels of comforts.

My military future did not look at all so unpromising as I had supposed it would be from the hardships of the first weeks.

At the beginning of October, after a period of severe training, we were on the eve of being sent to the front. My wife, on the invitation of my kind host, Herr Knippenberg, came to Ohrdruf to say good-bye. Another fortnight remained, however, during which the regiment was kept in readiness and we expected our marching orders at every parade.

Early on a beautiful autumn morning I was on parade when my company was cheered up by seeing my wife bring my weapon, which I had forgotten. "You would have gone off to war without your rifle," said she.

Among the young volunteers, mostly students, I was the only married man. After I had introduced my wife to my companions I still required some time before confessing I was a father. Then the child's portrait made the rounds, and the whole company awaited with me the arrival of his first tooth.

The regiment struck camp finally at the end of October. We were warned of it days in advance and I formed a double quartet from among my Aix companions with fine voices, who gave my wife a serenade of some beautiful old soldiers' songs. The question which of us nine musicians would return lay unspoken in our hearts and it was a good thing we did not know the answer. Herr Knippenberg sobbed into his waxed moustache and treated the singers and their friends to a farewell drink, at which the natural gaiety of youth triumphed over unpleasant thoughts. In the grey of the morning the regiment was loaded into goods trucks, and we journeyed for many days and nights to an unknown destination through a Germany still at that time enthusiastic for war.

Other people have told the story of the war better than I can, and the experiences of the young volunteer regiments in Flanders have been described often enough, so that I think I may be spared a repetition. I deliberately confine myself to telling as shortly as possible my own experiences.

After detraining at Thielt, a small town in the heart of Belgium, we immediately marched off without stopping there. We got to Rousselaere, a beautiful old Flemish town, the houses of which were already burning in many places. This first brought powerfully before our eyes the misery of war. In a street fight our company suffered its first death. It was that of a young man called Josefssohn.

A fine rain was falling and we received the order to bivouac in the fields in front of the town on the way to Ypres. Tired to death and ravenously hungry after a fatiguing march of several days, we fell on a splendid chicken broth when the order came for the regiment to form in three lines ready for action. We were to fix bayonets, throw ourselves on the wet earth at the appointed distances, and hold our tongues. No one knew what was going to happen, when a stout colonel on a heavy horse galloped up and drew rein in front of us.

He announced in a loud voice that contact with the enemy had been made and a cavalry attack against us, who formed the vanguard, was to be expected very soon. He described the situation clearly as it was reflected in his mind. He said: "I have divided the regiment into three lines. Each of these, which will be placed a hundred yards one behind the other, has a special task. The first will, of course, be ridden down, the second will stop the enemy, and the third will destroy him."

Now we knew! I was in the first line and had a few hours to picture to myself how being ridden down would work out in practice. Then it turned out that our whole fright had been merely a false alarm. A pity about the chicken broth!

The next morning we really had our first fight with the enemy's rearguard. Again we had to fix bayonets, and were ordered to charge a wood lying a few hundred yards in front of us. We rushed forward, cheering. I stumbled and fell on my own bayonet, which made a considerable cut in my left hand between thumb and first finger. The blood poured out and soaked my coat, on which I was pressing my hand. A comrade helped to bind it up while machine-gun bullets and shrapnel were falling around us.

The wounded who could not be treated in the field dressing-stations were taken to Aix, where they spread the rumour that Busch had a bad stomach wound. Through devious channels and in differing versions this news reached my wife who, with our six-months-old son, had remained with her parents at Mengeringhausen. She immediately prepared to go to Aix to put on foot investigations, but was relieved by a telegram. However, two days later she was thrown into fresh doubts by the arrival of a letter from official sources announcing the heroic death of her husband.

While the terror of this uncertainty dragged on for two weeks I was marching quite cheerfully with the troops, with no suspicion of the agitating results which my blood-stained coat had produced.

One evening we came to Poelcapelle, where we were to spend the night. After a wearisome march along a narrow road, in places rough, in places boggy, and so blocked up by artillery and other troops on the march that there was hardly room for the infantry, we could literally no longer stand on our legs. Many of us were left lying in the ditches on the way, and I myself only found it possible not to be left behind because on the last stretch I had tied myself with a strap to a gun limber and allowed myself to be dragged along by it. We had only one desire—sleep, sleep!

In Poelcapelle, in the middle of the night, we went stumbling over men who had thrown themselves down in the street and in every available place and seemed to have left not a square yard of room for those who came after them. No one suspected that scarcely a kilometre away in Langemarck the English and French were lying in similar conditions, likewise unaware of the state of affairs in Poelcapelle. How right Tolstoi was in *War and Peace* when he represented chance and not strategic judgment as the deciding factor in war!

I was delayed by a conversation with the Captain. Everything lay in profound sleep when I tried to find a free place in the church to rest my tired limbs for a few hours.

The church was stuffed just as full as the whole of Poelcapelle. Cursed by all the sleepers I was disturbing, I at last found a suitable place for a musician—in the organ gallery, where I immediately sank down and fell asleep. I slept so soundly that when I woke up, to my great alarm, I found the church empty. Hundreds of men had left without my noticing their noisy departure.

I found myself alone in the nave, which was already riddled

with shot, and ran off full of shame to find my good Captain and my company. At the outskirts of the village I reached them. They had already been told off in the usual three platoons. From my height I belonged to the first platoon. However, as the formation could not be upset, the Captain relegated me angrily to the position of last man at the end of the third platoon.

The assault of the young volunteer regiments on the gas factory of Langemarck, which has been described so often, began. The two first platoons of my company were sent in to this fight; the third platoon where, to my shame, I found myself, was ordered to stay in reserve for the time being, as escort for the artillery. After some hours the residue of the two platoons came back. The assault had been beaten off with great loss; many of my friends and companions had been killed or severely wounded. It was no doing of mine that sleep had saved my life or at least my limbs.

I was by no means happy about it that day. At that time danger did not count. It would have seemed cowardly and contemptible if anyone had cared for his own safety.

To make up for my sleepiness I applied to the Captain for permission to join a patrol that was not without danger. I pushed my way across a high-lying piece of ground that was under fire, crawled into a farmyard, scrambled up the chimney and tried to survey the battle. But our troops were streaming back in such confused masses that every endeavour to get a view of them was in vain.

In considerable disorder we turned back to Ostnieuwkerke, a village lying back a few kilometres, where we assembled for lunch. When we were standing in formation the Captain discovered that my bandolier and side arms were missing. I had lost them on the patrol. In view of this further "offence against service regulations" the Captain's patience gave way and he shouted at me: "A German soldier does not lose his equipment!" My timid explanations made no impression on him. He was furious with me and I with him.

In this mood I set out with the others once more towards Langemarck. As the enemy's shrapnel fire was becoming more and more violent and tearing great holes in our ranks, we dug ourselves in behind a hedge. We dug and dug to hide our heads in the ground and, if possible, the rest of the body. One took no heed of one's neighbour.

Suddenly I heard a Rhenish voice near me saying beseechingly: "I sang in the Aix choir under you and have always had such a respect for you. I'm so frightened. In the hour of danger may I say *du* to you?"[1]

"Of course, why not?" I called back. But it didn't do the poor devil much good. Half an hour later he was dead.

Oh, how nonsensical and criminal it all was! English Colonial soldiers were coming on us with fixed bayonets, standing proudly upright and without the slightest attempt to take cover. They were firing round me like mad. I raised my rifle, when I remembered that I had not got my bandolier and cartridges. Someone roared out: "There, beside you—there are some there!"[2] There lay *my* bandolier which I had lost! The luck of the battle had brought me back to the same square metre where I had lain in the morning.

That evening I ran into my Captain in Poelcapelle, which was burning and almost destroyed. Delighted to see me, he said:

"Thank God you are alive, Busch!"

I saluted smartly.

"Private Busch reporting with bandolier."[3]

"You are an ass," said the Captain. But we were good friends again.

Trench warfare, only interrupted by slight attacks, began. One day there suddenly appeared the same stout colonel who had already given us an unnecessarily sleepless night and had

[1] "Herr Musikdirector, ich hab bei Ihnen in Aachener Chor mitjesungen und hab Sie immer so verehrt. Ich hab so Augst. Darf ich in der Stunde der Jefahr nich du zu Ihnen sagen?"
[2] Fass neben dich, da liejen welche!
[3] Kriegsfreiwilliger Busch meldet sich gehorsamst mit Koppel zurück.

deprived us of a good chicken broth at Rousselaere. This time he ordered us to attack the trenches facing us. Our objection that our own troops were before us he declared was false and we were cowards. Brandishing his revolver in the air, he threatened to shoot us, and then ran panting to another place where he issued the same orders.

As we were without officers and left to ourselves, I took over the command of the trench in which we were lying concealed between two little streams. That is to say, I made them fix bayonets and ordered them all to jump out of the trench when I had counted three. The success of my military action was striking. When I had roared out "Three!" and "Hurrah!" I leapt out of the trench followed by *one* of my comrades. The others were smarter and stayed inside. A shot immediately shattered my companion's lower jaw. I myself fled to a shell hole full of water, where I served as a target for the enemy's machine guns till twilight.

I crawled back in the darkness and found Strauch lying unconscious in a clump of willows. I dragged him to the field dressing-station, and at the same time took the opportunity of having my wounded hand properly treated. Up to then I had paid no attention to it and it had got seriously worse.

When I returned from the field dressing-station I found the state of affairs in the trench had altered. They had succeeded in reassembling and re-forming the unit and in replacing the losses in officers and men. I lay in a hole in the ground once more with my former companions—at least, those who had survived the fight—and was dozing in a sort of half-sleep when I heard a musical voice near me. It came from an officer on inspection, and its slightly theatrical tone caught my ear. "If that is not an actor's voice," I thought, "then I have never been inside a theatre."

I raised myself and saw in front of me a Lieutenant-Colonel, a big, pleasant-looking man, who immediately called out: "For Heaven's sake, Busch, what are *you* doing here?" I also recognised him in a moment. He was called Grimm, yet that was not the name by which I first remembered him. Originally a professional officer, he left the service in due time as a Major, and when no longer young went on the stage on account of an actress, to whom he remained devoted throughout his life. At the outbreak of war he was recalled to the colours and was at that time Lieutenant-Colonel of my regiment. He was, it soon turned out, an excellent officer and, what is more to the point, a good, cultivated man who soon won the affection of those who were under him. In the course of the war he was wounded several times and on account of his achievements and personality deserved greater recognition than fell to his lot owing to his superiors' strange notions of morality.

When I first knew him it was under the name of Otto Provence. He was a member of a small theatrical company which played during the summer season at Bad Pyrmont. At that time we took many walks together and struck up a friendship. Now in the battlefield, I was merely a common private soldier, face to face with the officer in command of the regiment.

In the afternoon of the same day an orderly fetched me to the regimental headquarters. A haystack, a few hundred yards behind our trenches, served as cover for the dug-out in which the commanding officer and his adjutant lived. This lodging-place, primitive as it was, seemed to me, after camping in the trenches for weeks, a luxury hotel. I was made runner, so that I could remain in the neighbourhood of the staff in somewhat pleasanter living conditions. My new post was, however, by no means a cushy job; on the contrary. We orderlies had to maintain communications with the troops day and night over an open, unsheltered tract of ground always within range of the enemy's fire, and making use of every possible cover. When I took over this duty I shared it with five other men. After a few days there were only two of us left.

The trench warfare led to a pause in the fighting which continued at Langemarck till about April 1915 and, apart from small skirmishes and fights between patrols, was only once interrupted by a big action, in December 1914. For days violent artillery fire destroyed our communications behind the lines and part of the farmhouses which were still occupied; among them were the remains of the one where I and the rest of the regimental staff slept. French troops of an older class stormed the trenches held by my regiment. The poor devils stuck in the muddy surface water, so characteristic of the Flemish country-side, and were miserably destroyed.

Meanwhile the losses on the German side, especially among the officers, were considerable, and replacements were not to be expected as quickly as was desirable. Thus the Lieutenant-Colonel, on the day after this attack, handed over to me the command of the sixth company. He candidly told me that this promotion was due less to my military virtues than to a certain ability and experience in handling men in the mass. He expected above all that I should hold the position and keep up the morale of the troops.

One cold December night I waded out, accompanied by my batman, through trenches a yard deep in muddy water, to find my company. The section of troops entrusted to my care con-sisted of about sixty men who had dug themselves into the level ground of a potato field and were stuck in the water up to their stomachs. A frenzied artillery bombardment from the enemy began and destroyed a dam, which poured an additional stream into our trenches. Now we were standing in icy water up to our necks and were not afforded the slightest protection from the enemy's fire, which destroyed half the squad in my charge.

As all communication with the staff was impossible, when night fell I ordered a retreat of a few yards on my own respon-sibility, and we tried to make a new trench. But this attempt, too, was in vain. After the first cut with the spade the water gushed out of the earth and there was no possibility of making any defence or strengthening our position.

On the following night we were relieved and sent to a rest

camp at Ostnieuwkerke, about three kilometres distant. In normal conditions one could have got back there in half an hour, but on this night I needed four hours on the way, crawling for the most part on hands and knees, for after remaining in icy water for some fifty hours my body had no more strength in it.

My batman, who had not stayed behind in the trenches, had requisitioned a room for me in a partially ruined farmhouse and was waiting for me there. The occupants had fled, taking with them as many of their household goods as possible; but there was still a large copper which could be used for a bath. With the batman, parcels of comforts from home had arrived. Germany was still at that time a rich country whose wealth after the few months of war had been by no means consumed. I was overpowered by surprise and gratitude when I came upon twenty-five parcels of ten pounds each—two and a half hundredweight of gifts! They did not contain only the socks and mittens knitted by old ladies which we greeted with contempt, but also champagne, caviare, and other delicacies, besides pints of eau-de-cologne, as well as cigars, cigarettes and other treasures which for long we thought we had forgotten.

In an hour I had changed from an almost helpless animal-like creature hardly able to move and had become a man once more; silk underwear, new clothes, a clean shave, had restored me to civilisation, and as innumerable good books had also arrived I even felt that culture had returned.

I at once collected my closest battle companions who, like me, quickly forgot the misery of the last weeks after taking part in my superfluity. Comradeship was the strongest bond in war. This feeling survived the enthusiasm for war, which disappeared so quickly, and was for most of us the motive that made us carry on to the end. Soon we were no longer fighting for our country, for house and home, or whatever the catchword was. No, we fought not to leave our companions in the lurch.

The regiment had suffered too much not to be in need of a long period of rest and recovery. We thus came to the base at Rumbeke, a suburb of Rousselaere.

Our conception of recovery and that of the military authorities were very different. We could hardly stand upright before the merciless drill began which often made us feel a longing for the life of the trenches. To be sure I, personally, had a better time of it, as I received a commission in January 1915 and was finally confirmed as Company Commander of the sixth company.

In Rumbeke the General in command of our army corps had, with his staff, established his quarters in an idyllically situated *château* in the middle of a delightful park. On the evening of our arrival in the little town Lieutenant-Colonel Grimm and his Adjutant, a university professor, were invited to dinner. It turned out that the General was interested in music and I was ordered to go to the *château* the next evening.

Owing to my rapid promotion, my officer's uniform had not yet arrived, so that the Lieutenant-Colonel lent me a pair of trousers and the Adjutant a coat. After a detailed inspection by both gentlemen I was taken to the *château* in a gig.

The General was a good-natured, genial gentleman who spoke the Swabian dialect with a strong accent. After a first-rate dinner, though I was somewhat out of practice I played Beethoven's *Moonlight Sonata* and other things, after which the General, accompanied by his staff, then took me into an adjoining room. A batman brought another bottle of French champagne, there were Havana cigars, and life appeared to me in the rosiest light.

The General asked jovially about my war experiences and declared that for once he would like very much to hear from a front-line soldier a sincere criticism of how the war was carried on.

He thus fulfilled an ardent wish of my own. For some time I had been dreaming of an opportunity of speaking freely to someone in authority of what I had for long been thinking inwardly but could not utter aloud. The whole atmosphere—the champagne, the good cigars, the amiability of the hearty Swabian General and the obvious benevolence with which the

Fritz Busch in 1922

rather more sedate Chief-of-Staff considered me, all this contributed to loosen my tongue.

I glibly explained that our field artillery was worthless, that it constantly hit our trenches rather than the enemy's and, finally, had not been able to destroy a nest of enemy machineguns on our flank so that we had suffered unnecessary losses. I spoke of the failure of the pioneers who, instead of helping to dig trenches, had left us to rot for weeks in mud and water holes. I complained of bad provisions and other abuses.

In my eagerness I did not notice that the benevolent Chief-of-Staff was taking down my criticism in writing.

I closed my forcible statement with an invitation to the General sometime to visit *our* trenches, the only ones in which, thanks to the precautions of my commanding officer and the special proficiency of my fellow-soldiers, things were after all as far as possible what they ought to be. The General accepted with thanks.

Enraptured with the delightful evening I got home late. Only a few hours later, about six in the morning, I was summoned before the officer commanding the regiment. He was already sitting at breakfast with the Adjutant and was curious to hear more about my visit to the *château*. I gave a detailed report and added proudly that I had succeeded in persuading the General to visit the regiment as soon as we should be in trenches again.

Lieutenant-Colonel Grimm turned pale. The Adjutant discreetly left the room. Grimm, rising to his full height and holding the top of the table firmly with both hands, shouted out: "Good God! are you out of your mind? Don't you know, you ——"—here came several epithets I cannot repeat—"that every officer's first effort should be to keep his superiors away? These gentry have to justify their existence; as it is they stick their noses into everything that doesn't concern them. A visit from one of them always leads to trouble. For months I have been avoiding it in every possible way. And now, unlucky wretch, you go and give the old fool a special invitation!"

Utterly overcome, the poor fellow fell back in his chair. I stood in front of him turned to stone. Suddenly he got up and shouted: "Take off your trousers, idiot! If only I hadn't been such an ass as to lend them to you! You wouldn't have run off there in your pants, you . . . you . . ."

He gestured with his hand to me not to speak. He sat silent for a long time, his head sunk on his breast. Then, somewhat more composed, he said: "Get yourself invited again and talk the General out of the visit. *How* you do that is your business; but take care that I don't set eyes on the fellow."

I went to my quarters, where I already found a summons to go to dinner again that evening at the *château*. The hardest part of my task had thus solved itself. Now the problem was to disinvite the General.

Finally, I asked for advice from two staff officers who had been present the day before and explained to them frankly what I had done. Both of them advised me laughingly to let drop to the General, in the course of conversation, that there were lice and rats in the trenches. Bullets and shells did not frighten him but the idea of such vermin terrified him.

It is true that up to then I had never seen a rat in our trenches and never discovered a louse, but now, after dinner, I had a menagerie of them marched up. I succeeded so well that the Adjutant shook himself with disgust and immediately ordered a sufficient quantity of insect powder and strychnine to exterminate the pests, to be placed at the disposal of the Infantry Reserve Regiment 236. The results should be reported. He would put off his visit to a time when the plague should have entirely disappeared.

Henceforth we took care to have always at hand a small stock of rats and a collection of lice.

To the position of company commander was attached the use of a horse. Owing to this, a good part of the enjoyment of my new dignity was lost. Horses are remarkable animals. Provided by nature with four legs, they seem usually to make use of only two, while they raise the other two in the air. Anyone who has as little sporting talent as I, has good reason to fear them. They put me on a young horse straight from the remounts, and the staff officer who taught riding, and whom I knew from my visits to the *château*, picked me out to lead the cavalcade.

One often hears that animals are more intelligent than men. In any case, the problem of free will was no problem for my horse. This horse *had* free will, which he knew how to show clearly after I had got on his back. He could not endure me, ran away and threw me. Repeated attempts led to the same result and finally made me unfit for service for a long time.

While the regiment returned to its position in the line, I was left to the care of my batman at Rumbeke. A strange regiment took up its quarters in the small town and I was left to my own thoughts so far as I was not busied with the harmless occupation of billeting officer which had been handed over to me.

An official letter from the Division unexpectedly disturbed my idyllic life. It ran:

"Your Honour[1] recently, in a personal interview with His Excellency the General in Command, made various criticisms on the conduct of the war by the 26th Reserve Corps. As the divisional commander does not understand what were your Honour's intentions in expressing these criticisms your Honour is herewith requested to give, within twelve hours, an exact report, attaching thereto a sketch-map," etc., etc.

The above-mentioned Divisional Commander under our Corps Commander was a General von K., who stood high in the favour of Kaiser Wilhelm. Whether it were the antagonism between North and South which made the Prussian junker hateful to the Swabian aristocrat or whatever it was, the fact remains that His Excellency von H. and General von K. were like cat and dog together. To the Swabian it was a peculiar satisfaction to give the Prussian an unexpected blow by handing

[1] Euer Hochwohlgeboren.

on to him my sharp criticism of the state of affairs at the front of his Division.

What a sketch-map was I knew pretty well; but to know how to make one was not one of my gifts. My batman, who had already helped me out of many sticky places, was a bright youth from Cologne-Nippes, and had learnt the trade of shoe-maker. He understood the art of drawing as little as I did. In this desperate situation I thought of the advice of an older fellow-soldier: always to make such productions for one's superiors as colourful as possible, and to use a ruler. I therefore bought a ruler as well as a great number of coloured pencils and went to work. The result was a compound of different styles and epochs. The lack of perspective it shared with old Chinese woodcuts; from the French impressionists I took the *pointilliste* technique; to show the terrain, which I no longer saw clearly before me, I made use of Rembrandt's *chiaroscuro*. In addition, I drew lines with my ruler. In twelve hours the work was finished and delivered.

Many days of anxiety followed. Meanwhile the division seemed to have lost all interest in me and to have given up the hope of obtaining from "his Honour" anything of any military value. They had other troubles, for the first gas attack was being prepared. I went through it in March or April 1915 and will say nothing about its horrible effects.

Being under canvas for weeks in the damp soil of Flanders was not without its effect on my health. I developed an inflammation of the nerves and was sent back to Germany for treatment. On the return from Ypres my brother-in-law clapped me on the shoulder in the Mengeringhausen railway station and said: "Yes, yes, the proverb is right: it's the best men who fall."

I went for several months to the hospital in Aix, then to another health resort, without curing my painful condition. After different medical boards had examined me at three-monthly intervals for a year I was finally declared unfit for military service.

But this did not mean a discharge from the army but only

116

garrison duty in the small towns of central Germany. Meanwhile I was still the Musikdirektor of Aix, only away on war service, and was frequently given leave from military duties to carry on my work there.

This western frontier town, so near the seat of operations that one could often hear clearly the thunder of the guns, had instituted thirty-six military hospitals, and the need for music and the wish for higher spirits, or perhaps only for escape from the lasting effects of alarm, were especially strong there. I conducted concerts, frequently for the Red Cross and other war purposes. At the end of the year 1917 I undertook, with the Aix Choral Society, a concert tour for front-line soldiers which brought us to the neighbourhood of Ypres. At Lille, Douai, Cambrai and Brussels we performed Haydn's *Seasons*.

In April 1916 I played with Max Reger at a chamber-music *soirée* the Beethoven *Variations* and the *Passacaglia* for two pianos without suspecting this was the last appearance of my friend, the great master. Four weeks later I read, in the officers' mess at Rudolstadt, the news of his sudden death. Only eight days previously I had visited him at Jena in his house, the acquisition of which had made him so proud. Apart from my personal loss I felt Reger's death as the greatest blow contemporary creative music could experience.

At Reger's cremation, Adolf and I played the Largo from the last violin and piano Sonata in C minor. The words came into my mind that Grillparzer had written for the tombstone of Franz Schubert: "Death here buried a rich treasure, but richer hopes."

I returned to my duties in the small garrison town. The soldiers' existence there often reminded me of the fairy tale of Hänsel and Gretel. The soldier was cherished by the witch, the state, nursed and fattened as far as the already noticeable restrictions allowed until he was ready to be eaten—that is, sent to the front as cannon fodder. My physical condition did not allow the "faith healers"—those medical boards which regularly combed out the garrison towns and wrote down all those who were even half-fit as fit for service in the front line—to offer me new opportunities of a hero's death. In the third year of the war "a hero's death" was no longer the desire of any soldier of normal feelings.

My experience of war brought me to recognise the political lies in which all who were responsible for the 1914 war had taken part either more or less. In the garrison I was employed with others as propaganda officer and I was given statistical information as to the success of the U-boat war and similar matters to study. This material I had to work up into regular lectures which I had to deliver to all those who belonged to the regiment who either had not been sent to the front again or could only be used on garrison duty. My success was very inconsiderable. I did not believe what I related to my subordinates who attended these lectures by order, nor did my men, for the most part Thuringian craftsmen or Rhineland miners, who, with the common sense of simple people, had already been feeling for some time that the military situation was not as favourable as their Lieutenant had to depict it. I was happy when these hours, so senseless and painful to me, were over, and I could either sit down at my piano again or bury myself in musical scores and books.

I asked myself whether there would be any sense, if things should again come to that point, in staking my life, career and work for ideals which, during the course of the war, had come to appear more and more questionable.

In a neutral country there was a colleague of mine, even years later so enthusiastic about war that he once told Busoni he composed much better and with more feeling since he had spent some time as colonel on active service in defence of his country. Busoni replied with melancholy humour: "According to that, how very differently Beethoven would have composed if he had been at least a corporal!"

Chapter Seven

STUTTGART

*As soon as you have confidence in
yourself you know how to live.*

GOETHE. FAUST

IN the spring of 1918, when I was a lieutenant at Gera, hear-
ing that Max von Schillings had retired from directing the
Stuttgart Court Opera, I applied for the position to the
Generalintendant,[1] von Putlitz. What decided me to take this
step was principally a certain artistic curiosity as to opera.
From the trifling experience I had had in this sphere I could
hardly reckon on success among the very numerous applicants.
To my great astonishment I received a telegram inviting me to
Stuttgart for a personal interview.

My reception by Putlitz was characteristic of the way things
were managed in those days, when the sovereign used to hand
over the exclusive responsibility of the management of the
court theatres he supported to one single individual in whom
he had confidence. The conversation I had with Putlitz in his
elegant room at the court theatre lasted hardly more than five
minutes. My offer of a trial performance as a guest conductor
was rejected as unnecessary and I became the Royal Württemberg Hof Kapellmeister.

Back in the hotel I felt as if I was hardly in my right senses.
I telegraphed for my wife with all speed, and we wandered
through Stuttgart together. The hilly Swabian town pleased
us extremely, not so the opera.

In the evening we attended a performance of *Traviata*. The
impression we received from it was characteristic of our atti-

[1] The official responsible for the artistic and administrative duties of a
State Opera House or Theatre. Before the revolution this official was
generally an important aristocrat.

tude at that time, which was prejudiced in favour of absolute music. We were not only disappointed at the low level of the repertory performance which was suffering from war-time deficiencies; the spirit of the work itself horrified us. It appeared to us trivial. Father Germont's Aria in the second act finally had such a ludicrous effect on us that we left the theatre in dismay.

On the way home we heard, through a half-open church door, the Benedictus from Beethoven's *Missa Solemnis*. I was seized with such violent nostalgia for the "pure" music I had been familiar with from my childhood that I repented of the step by which I had bound myself to opera as if I had sold my soul to the devil.

In all seriousness we had to be careful not to do anything rashly but wait until we had given opera a fair trial.

I am still giving it a trial to-day.

After the old Stuttgart theatre had been burnt down the Baron von Putlitz had succeeded, even before the first world war, in getting from the theatre-loving King and other friends of art, funds to build two theatres—a big one and a small one. Both buildings were among the most beautiful of German theatres, from their architectural style and their happy situation in the courtly atmosphere of the well-tended park of the old Castle.

The court orchestra was on the whole of an average quality. But in the leader, Carl Wendling, a pupil of Joachim's, it possessed a quite outstanding musician. Wendling had been among other things leader of the Meiningen court orchestra and of the Boston Symphony Orchestra, and had besides been summoned by Hans Richter to Bayreuth and there played for many years as leader of the first violins. I am grateful to this serious, cultivated and lovable man; my intercourse with him and our exchange of ideas enriched my years at Stuttgart. To hear that this liberal-minded man lived up to his principles in the later evil times was a satisfaction but no surprise.

The chief service that my predecessor, Max von Schillings,

had rendered the Stuttgart opera was the cultivated atmosphere which he had known how to create in this theatre. It was owing to his efforts that an outstanding company of singers was at hand—Helene Wildbrunn, Sigrid Hoffmann-Onegin, George Meader, the American tenor, and Karl Oestvig the Norwegian, to name only a few.

When I conducted my first opera, *Tristan and Isolde*, I had the pleasure of finding that, as at a previous symphony concert, public opinion approved of Putlitz's hasty choice.

Apart from the happy consciousness of the sympathy which I had for Stuttgart and which was shown me in the town from the first days to the last, the beginnings of my work there were not under the luckiest star. The war was approaching its sorry end; the terrible "Spanish 'flu" suddenly appeared and snatched away many lives in the course of a day, in Stuttgart as elsewhere. A universal apathy, the uncertainty of everyone whether he would be alive the next day, combined with the wretched economic conditions and the distressing scarcity of food produced to begin with a cheerless atmosphere to work in.

At the beginning of November 1918 the producer H. and I made an experiment at the suggestion of Appia the scene-painter, who lived in Geneva. We tried, in a new production of Wagner's *Rheingold*, to utilise the new lighting projector which up to then had hardly come into use. Our electrician, naturally enough, had not mastered the technique, which was new to him, so that the castle of the gods, which should have been projected on to the cyclorama in the shape of a pointed cone, at the first performance stood on its head, the apex undermost, the base at the top. In addition, Valhalla tottered visibly, which was not exactly helpful for the success of our novelty.

A further experiment, which as far as I know was made for the first time, was to put three ballet girls into the swimming apparatus, while the Rhine maidens who were to sing remained concealed behind a rock. The ballet dancers, who had been thoroughly coached in the music, imitated the singing and indicated the words with their lips, while bravely turning somersaults in the Rhine, to make the deception credible. This break with tradition in no way pleased the critic of an important newspaper. He wrote: ". . . and thus they certainly sang with their mouths but the sound came from the opposite side." The *Kladderadatsch*, a well-known very witty, satirical paper, commented very drastically on this unfortunate criticism.

In the dress rehearsal of this performance of *Rheingold*, Putlitz and I unexpectedly came into violent conflict. I waited for a long time in vain for the lights in the auditorium to be put out as usual, and finally was informed that by the wish of the Queen the house lights were to remain on, so that the great lady might have the opportunity of inspecting the audience. Horrified, I reproached him, pointing out Wagner's instructions to the contrary. Putlitz jumped up and spat out at me: "Perhaps *you* will persuade Her Majesty to sacrifice her wishes?"

"With the greatest pleasure," I returned. "Please procure me an audience at once—to-day."

Putlitz persisted indignantly: "You will have no luck." And raising his voice: "The house lights will remain on till the curtain goes up."

"And I, Your Excellency, will leave the house unless it is completely dark before the beginning of the first note."

At this dramatic moment there appeared as a *deus ex machina* the November revolution which put a stop to interviews with inquisitive queens.

Unfortunately, Putlitz, with whom I had been on the best of terms, socially and professionally, until this dispute, also gave up his appointment. As an aristocrat, he felt bound to his king by the word he had given, and consequently would not serve the new régime in spite of his strongly liberal inclinations.

My new superiors were completely congenial, and the form of government, so far as it did not interfere with artistic interests, was indifferent to me. Of course, the fate of my country could not be a matter of indifference to me, any more than to other decent Germans. The lost war, the universal misery that followed, grieved and embittered me as much as and perhaps more than many others. The difference between me and the great majority of my countrymen lay in the interpretation and judgment of the fundamental causes which had led to this lamentable state of affairs. During the war, into which I had been drawn, credulous and even enthusiastic, I had begun to think them over. I saw them in the domination of certain cliques and castes which found their profit or their irresponsible pleasures in war. If November 1918, after the first serious eruptions were over, promised to bring about a social revolution and a truly democratic form of government, I was in complete agreement with it.

At first, after the departure of Putlitz, the opera producer Dr. H. and I had to carry through an interregnum with the different councillors[1] which those years brought with them. Among them, to my no small astonishment, Dr. H., who until the outbreak of the revolution had been closely connected with the family of His Excellency Baron von Putlitz, suddenly made his appearance as a member of the Social-Democrat party. He wore their badges with obvious pride. At the next change in the state of affairs his docility was to surprise me. I found H., who had been summoned to Berlin, in an S.A. uniform in March 1933, marching at the head of a company. He was one of those opportunists who "had already followed the red flag when as yet there was no swastika on it."

Württemberg had always been reckoned a democratic country. The party which had now reached power, whose members were chiefly collected from teachers, trade union secretaries and members of the proletariat, laid great stress— as was soon to be observed—on not appearing the enemies of culture. The officials in the different ministries were to a great extent taken over. Among them was a Geheimrat von J., who was associated with the Social-Democrat Heymann, the Minister for Fine Arts, as his right hand in matters dealing with the theatre. He faced the complicated affairs of opera without the

[1] "Räten" in the original text.

slightest comprehension, and therefore conscientiously demanded report after report on the most trivial transactions. For the real object of the theatre—namely, to have good performances—there was consequently no time. One day I lost patience and set before him the resultant ill effects in what seemed to me a conclusive fashion. When I had finished, the Geheimrat gave me a friendly look through his spectacles and said: "It's all very interesting, sir, what you say. Now make me a report about it!"[1]

The staff of the theatre finally chose "a man in whom they had confidence" who was not a man in whom I had confidence. I was therefore in the theatre from early morning to late at night. I once overheard on the dark stage two scene-shifters who were discussing me. In pure Swabian dialect I heard:

"You know, he must be unhappily married, he's never at home."[2]

The Württemberg Theatre was in more and more pressing need of the strong hand of a Generalintendant. Innumerable candidates were interested in this position. In order to avoid any premature public announcement all concerned were on their honour to preserve complete silence—and this applied to the Berne Intendant, Albert Kehm, who came to Stuttgart for a conference in complete secrecy. The intervention of any theatrical agency had been excluded with especial care.

Kehm went from the station to the Hotel Marquardt to dress for his visit to the minister. While he was sitting in his bath there came a knock. Through a chink in the door peered the well-known face of the theatrical agent, Frankfurter.

"Well, how did I manage this?" he asked.

It must be admitted that the achievement was worth the ten per cent which the new Intendant had to pay him for the next few years.

Gradually, after the agitations of the revolution, quieter con-

---

[1] "Dees isch eisserschd inderessand, Herr Landesmusigdiregder, was Sie mir do alles erzält habe. Etz macher Sie amol an Bericht."

[2] "Weisch, der moss ohglicklich verheiradet sei', der isch jo nie z'haus."

ditions prevailed. The concert hall which until then had served as a military hospital was no longer obliged to waste its splendid acoustics in echoing the cries of human sufferers. It was divested of its doleful aroma of chloroform and was prepared in friendly fashion to serve the Muses once more. Now, as always after a war, though material deficiencies persisted, the need for good art became all the greater.

Everyone in Stuttgart can remember that at the opening of the subscription for the twelve yearly symphony concerts the enthusiastic, practical Swabians, in their enthusiasm for music, once brought some camp beds with them which they put at night in front of the booking office so as to be on the spot in good time in the morning.

In the neighbouring little town of Mühlacker a well-to-do Jewish friend of the place had a festival hall built which possessed a complete modern stage so that we could produce *Figaro* and *Fidelio*. Over the entrance to the hall which he had given to his fellow-citizens at the time of the Versailles treaty, the enthusiastic music lover and patriot had had engraved the word "Nevertheless".

"Nevertheless" some twenty years later he and his wife and daughter found themselves in a concentration camp.

In Freudenstadt, a health resort in the Württemberg Black Forest, a theatre was built, thanks to the initiative of two lovers of art—the cultivated mayor, Blaicher, and the energetic hotel proprietor Erwin Lutz. In this theatre the Stuttgart Opera Company was able to give guest performances. Of course it was often necessary to take the will for the deed there. The auditorium and stage had been built, in those hard times, on such a modest scale that in *Fidelio* the decidedly corpulent Leonora on her entry in the dungeon scene upset the earthenware jug in which Erwin Lutz had placed a litre of good Baden wine to strengthen and rejoice the thirsty Florestan.

Among the frequent visitors to the little theatre were President Ebert and Gerhart Hauptmann, who often took rooms in Lutz's Waldeck Hotel. Day after day one could see Gerhart

Hauptmann who, as author of *The Weavers*, was particularly honoured and loved by the new republic, in eager conversation with the clever and serious president, walking to and fro in the beautiful paths of the Black Forest. No one could imagine at that time that those who held freedom dear were to be disillusioned in Hauptmann as well.

In 1922 Ebert,[1] on one of his visits to Freudenstadt, was to have a dinner given in his honour which the Württemberg ministers were to attend. When the little festivity took place Ebert himself was not there. At midday the news of the assassination of Rathenau had arrived and was a crushing blow to the already suffering president. We had occasion to admire the composure and restraint of Frau Ebert, who appeared at table and took the place of her sick husband with natural dignity. Seldom have jeers and arrogance, attempting to make a woman of modest origins ridiculous, chosen a more unsuitable target than Luise Ebert.

In Swabia, and especially in its capital, Stuttgart, in times of the greatest poverty there prevailed an intense intellectual life. The most fruitful feelings of good fellowship remained unimpaired during the times of poverty and sorrow that followed the war. There was contact with outstanding representatives of other arts, such as Kokoschka and Poelzig, members of the Dessau Bauhaus, with authors and members of the local Stuttgart publishing firms. Although they did not in general possess the natural musical gifts of, for instance, the Viennese or Rhinelanders, the Swabians, from their wide talents and intellectual activity, possessed an adaptability that offered a welcome to music even when it was difficult to approach and off the beaten track.

Kehm, the Intendant, as well as Dr. Otto Ehrhardt, the new opera producer, was a great admirer of Hans Pfitzner, who had attained the chief success of his life with the first performance of his *Palestrina* under Bruno Walter at Munich. The work was accepted for Stuttgart.

[1] Friedrich Ebert, first President of the German republic.

The composer was known as a difficult character. I really knew more about his controversial writings, often on the boundary line of bitterness, and his many eccentricities, than of his musical works, which did not specially appeal to me after a hasty study. But *Palestrina*, in spite of many uninteresting passages, made a great impression on me. We had a good cast at our disposal and awaited the arrival of the celebrated composer with eager expectation.

This expectation was fully gratified. Hans Pfitzner showed himself to be the man who had been described to us; dissatisfied with everything, offended directly anyone opened his mouth, and, although advanced in years, after the first rehearsal regularly in love with whatever actress might be taking the part of the young Ighino, Palestrina's son. According to his custom, he drove the theatre personnel to despair by coming too early to unprepared rehearsals. In spite of these peculiarities we did not lose our enjoyment of the beautiful work and *Palestrina* was a complete success at Stuttgart too.

During the following summer, at Pfitzner's property on the Ammersee, I discussed with him the possibility of producing his *Rose vom Liebesgarten*. After the Stuttgart success he received me in as friendly a way as was possible to him and offered to play the whole work through to me on the piano that same night. Various guests who were to be present would, he assured me, be delighted to hear him execute it, and I could undertake the vocal parts.

Now, I must confess that it is *not* one of the joys of my profession to listen to composers strumming their works to me on the piano. They are usually more enthusiastic about their powers of execution than I am. I like to hear careful piano playing but prefer to look over a score quietly at home and examine its worth. As I was sure of my good sight reading, I proposed to Pfitzner that I myself should play the unknown opera on the piano, while he should undertake the voice parts.

Pfitzner bleated out suspiciously: "But unfortunately you don't know the work at all!"

I declared confidently that I would pay him ten *pfennige* for every wrong note I played in the course of the evening.

All went well till about page 40, when Pfitzner in an excited passage turned over too late. I could not grasp a complicated chord with several double sharps quickly enough, and struck powerfully the notes that lay in the neighbourhood.

Pfitzner immediately caught my arm firmly. "There! Now you owe me one mark fifty," he said snappishly.

I thoroughly understood Pfitzner's caustic humour. Richard Strauss once said of him, with heartless wit: "If he finds it such a burden why does he compose?"

In the following years I conducted many works of Pfitzner's, concertos as well as operas, and felt respect for the seriousness and sincerity of his creative work, while I did not agree with the opinions which he laid down in many writings.

For reasons which are not worth telling, we later quarrelled violently and the ten years' connection between two fundamentally different natures was broken up.

The Swabians had a predilection for Anton Bruckner—in particular his slow movements fell in to a great extent with their feeling for what is mystic and profound. The audiences at my concerts were wholeheartedly in agreement with the idea of organising a Bruckner Festival. Shortly afterwards, when we repeated the seventh symphony in the Swabian university town of Tübingen, the enthusiasm, especially of the young students, knew no bounds. The Students' Association *Normannia* invited me to a convivial meeting, which proved the accuracy of a pretty verse on the intellectual powers of the Swabian race: "Schiller and Hegel, Uhland and Hauff, such men are the rule with us and strike no one as strange."[1]

The young freshers were ordered by the chairman during the merry-making to make each one in five minutes a couplet

---

[1] Der Schiller und der Hegel,
Der Uhland und der Hauff,
dees isch bei uns die Regel
dees fallet keinem auf.

128

on "Busch and Music" and sing it to a well-known tune. I awarded the prize to a philosophically minded budding Schiller who sang with a rough voice but plenty of conviction:

Herr Busch, who seems all hearts to win,
Can really only make a din.[1]

I myself was only a young man, hardly past thirty. I felt completely at one with young people and was glad when I could co-operate with them. At a guest performance at Frankfort I noticed in the opera orchestra a young violinist who played with spirit. I found that he was called Hindemith and composed modern music. I took his first operas to give them performances at Stuttgart. They were operas in one act, amongst them one with the remarkable title, *Murder, Hope of Women*, suggestive of many plays on the words. The book was by the painter Kokoschka. The two other one-act operas with words by Franz Blei and another librettist of expressionist tendencies, were called *Nusch-Nuschi* and *Sancta Susanna*.

Although I was not lacking in the courage to defy the guardians of sacred traditions, I did not venture to accept the latter of the three works owing to its obscenity. We kept to the two first, and the scandal caused by their performance was quite enough to make me avoid the open anger which the third opera would undoubtedly have caused.

Hope, Murder of Women, or rather, *Women, Murder of Hope*—perhaps one might say *Women, Hope of Murder*? No, no, *Murder, Hope of Women*, this collaboration between a highly-gifted inventive painter and a very talented musician, slipped by with no special excitement, probably because no one realised what actually happened in the piece. On the other hand, the action in *Nusch-Nuschi* was easy enough to take in. The favourite wife of a Maharajah was smitten by the charms of a general who was in supreme command of her husband's

---

[1] Herr Busch, für den sie alle schwärmen
Tut doch im Grunde nichts als lärmen!

troops, and his most trusted friend. When the Prince discovered what had happened he commanded in the greatest wrath that the traitor should be punished by losing his manhood. Violently depicted in the orchestra, this, God be praised, took place behind the scenes. But after that, when the fat general was dragged on to the stage by the bodyguard and had to face the deeply reproachful look of the Prince, a solo trombone in the orchestra quoted King Mark's words in *Tristan and Isolde*: "To me, Tristran, this . . . this, Tristran, to me!"[1]

Now the Swabians were not prudes, and especially at that time, when after a war much was permissible, were not narrow-minded where dramatic events were concerned. On the other hand, they were completely lacking in tolerance—and I must now say quite rightly—to make them put up with an insult to their most sacred treasures, as they understood the quotation from *Tristan* to be. There was a scandal which increased the more when the newspapers attacked the affair, and public opinion denounced the guilty one. I myself was the guilty one and I admitted it.

In reality the whole business was a storm in a teacup. It was forgiven and forgotten the quicker that it could not be denied that my directing of opera had more positive results. Richard Wagner's demand: "Children, create what is new!" was satisfied by performances of contemporary composers such as Busoni, Schreker, Braunfels, Schoeck, which went off more favourably than in the case of the young Hindemith. Looking round among other less known older works I came on *Boris Godunow*, which an earlier isolated attempt had not made at home on the German stage. In Stuttgart it achieved success in spite of a decided mistake in the production to which I shall return later. This success lasted, and later was followed by the Dresden production, famous at home and abroad. Above all, however, by careful and loving performances I had rectified my over-hasty and quite false judgment on Verdi, whom I learnt to recognise as one of the greatest dramatic musicians.

[1] Mir dies, Tristan . . . dies, Tristan, mir.

The new Stuttgart productions of *Il Trovatore*, *Othello* and *Falstaff* laid the foundations of a Verdi revival which, starting in Dresden, shortly afterwards influenced opera repertory all over Germany.

We were happy in Stuttgart and felt that we had taken root there. Nature and man, the way of life of the country—everything alike seemed full of promise to us. We often remembered the horribly rainy night when we finally moved in, if only at first to furnished rooms. (Aix was still in the hands of the army of occupation and it was to be long before the Belgians gave up our own possessions, all intact, apart from a frightful picture of Kaiser Wilhelm with a waxed moustache which I had received as a school prize. I shed no tears over its destruction.)

On the long road from the station, which had then to be traversed on foot, we thought uneasily, while the icy raindrops whipped our faces, of the unfamiliar, cold house towards which we with our tired little boy were struggling. However, a miracle awaited us. Kind people had lit the stoves and made the beds. Christmas gifts, then difficult to obtain, had been piled up for us. From them were hanging cards with names of people we hardly knew or, indeed, did not know at all. They bade us welcome. From that night we loved Stuttgart.

The Alsatian Tavern, an unusual sort of inn, was a refuge in time of need, a resort of friendly meetings for a large circle after the opera or concerts, or for intimate conversation in one of the cosy little nooks provided with tables. The proprietor, Ernst Widmann, a man passionately devoted to the theatre, had been a professional magician and he still practised magic. He not only allowed the guests to see from time to time to their great delight the most astonishing exhibitions from the realm of magic. He was a complete master of this difficult technique and could reproduce the well-known live rabbit out of a hat. He also worked his magic on dead pigs and other pleasures of the table at that time in short supply.

It cannot be denied that a certain partiality was shown in the Alsatian Tavern. Anyone could be sure of this when the waitress called out her order at the counter. This was either "A chop!" or "A chop for the theatre!" which was significant. If, however, one heard "A chop for the Generalmusikdirektor!" that meant something worth seeing.

Even if the world was topsy-turvy, the kind and friendly Widmann supported by his charming wife knew how to conjure up comfort, and made us feel at home in a way which we can never forget.

It was delightful in Stuttgart. The liberal convictions which hardly allowed one to feel a difference of creed or caste as one did in other parts of Germany created a happy atmosphere of freedom and cordiality such as we never found again in any other German town. But it was still too soon, I myself was too far from the age of discretion, still too young and restless to be able to settle down. My life and work had so far run in a smooth ascent without special difficulties; great troubles and hard battles were still to come.

For the winter of 1921 I was invited to give a concert with the State Orchestra at Dresden.

Some eighty years earlier Richard Wagner as Hofkapellmeister of Saxony had introduced regular series of symphony concerts in the Dresden Opera House. Since the death of Ernst von Schuch they had been latterly directed by Fritz Reiner. In the course of time opposition to him arose, as is often the case, so that the orchestra managing board invited many guest conductors, among them myself, for the winter of 1921–1922.

At the Dresden main station, in spite of the very early hour of the morning, I was solemnly received by six gentlemen of the orchestra managing board. They accompanied me to a hotel for breakfast, at which two speeches were delivered. The first, made to me, dealt with the honour which had fallen to me in conducting such a famous orchestra, which went back over four hundred years to the time of Martin Luther. In the second, I replied that I would take all possible pains not to disappoint such an illustrious body.

In the orchestra pit of the magnificent Opera House I found assembled to receive me the whole State Orchestra, a hundred and twenty-seven musicians. The members who were not taking part sat and listened in the stalls and I began with the Second Symphony of Brahms.

When, after an hour and a half of intense work, I ended the excellent rehearsal, the members of the managing board followed me into the green-room to deliver a third speech. Its upshot was that the orchestra had just resolved unanimously to hand over to me the direction of their six concerts for the future, if I would do them the honour to take charge of them.

In spite of many experiences with different orchestras I could not resist a feeling of special happiness and excitement in this rehearsal. The Dresden orchestra enjoyed the undisputed fame of being one of the best orchestras in the world. The mere wealth of its proportions aroused astonishment—besides a big body of strings, six of each woodwind, so many brass players that I counted twelve horns, I was surprised by a beauty of tone I had never heard before and an outstanding bowing technique in the strings which I have hardly found so complete in any other orchestra.

In the few days between this first rehearsal and the concert I saw that in towns with a strongly marked musical culture the success of an artist can be decided long before his public appearance and without actual proof or support from the press. From the first, a peculiar atmosphere of anticipation and sympathy was created, a growing excitement which on the evening of the concert let itself go in the enthusiasm of a full house.

Like a drunken man, I went back to Stuttgart after this first Dresden concert, the splendid sound of the orchestra ringing in my ears.

Reger, the practical man, once said to me: "There is only one proof of a real success. One must be re-engaged at once!" If he was right I had reason to be satisfied with the Dresden success. Along with the orchestra, the opera director, Scheidemantel, formerly a celebrated singer, had come to me to offer me the post of Generalmusikdirektor of the Dresden State Opera.

Shortly before, I had agreed to a contract of several years with Stuttgart, and we were attached to the town.

For some weeks I consoled myself with the idea of a compromise. I would conduct the Dresden symphony concerts during the holidays which were included in my contract. I would refuse the Opera and would continue to live in Stuttgart. Then, after my second concert in Dresden, Count Seebach, the former Generalintendant of the Saxon Court Theatre, made his appearance and took part in the affair, more cleverly than was agreeable to me.

Seebach told me that he was extremely interested in my coming to Dresden but only if I undertook the Opera at the same time. With this intention he had in the meantime decided the Saxon government to take over the control of the six symphony concerts which had been in the hands of the orchestra for many decades. In this way the right of the orchestra to choose a conductor was abolished and given to the government. The government wished to appoint only a kapellmeister who was also willing to undertake the Opera.

I at once realised that Count Seebach did not lack the power to carry through his wishes. In Dresden at this time the interregnum was still carrying on in which, as formerly in Stuttgart, the members of the Labour Party interested themselves without much success in the fate of the theatre. Although no longer in office, the Count still had sufficient authority to point out what he thought was right behind the scenes to those who could make decisions and thus to attain the results he wished for.

Seebach called himself a child of the theatre and maintained that it had only been a question of moments that he had not come into the world in a box of the Paris Opera. His father had been that Saxon ambassador who in his sixtieth year showed Richard Wagner in exile many long continued acts of friendship, and to my knowledge took much trouble over his return to Germany. Passionately interested in the opera, the mother of my Count Seebach had gone to the Paris Opera immediately before her confinement to be present at a performance of *Tannhäuser*, when her first pains forced her to return home with all speed.

The child of the theatre grew to be a man of great size in every sense, including the physical. A visitor once came to his study; Seebach offered him a chair which, in spite of several invitations, he refused. When the Count, rather annoyed, said: "But do finally sit down!" he received the answer: "Impossible, as long as Your Excellency is standing." "But I *am* sitting," cried the Count in despair.

He had a sense of humour, great experience, and superior intelligence. With unusual skill, with affection and understanding for the welfare of those who worked for him, broadminded and full of insight, for many years he controlled both the Dresden Opera and the Theatre. We often regretted that we could not work together, since Seebach, just like Putlitz, gave up his position in consequence of the November revolution. For a long time—"you cannot stop the silkworm from spinning"—he was present in the director's box at every big opera event and often even on ordinary repertoire nights. He left now and then to have a pull at his beloved cigarette. As smoking inside the theatre was strictly forbidden, he betook himself to the unlighted passageway between the auditorium and the stage, where, on a stone floor, there was a tall chest full of sand. Anyone going by often saw the light of a cigarette glimmering in the darkness, and Seebach, with his elegant, incredibly long legs, half leaning, half sitting on the chest. At the end of the performance, innumerable cigarette ends could be found there.

In spite of the difference in age between us of about forty years we were good friends and our friendship lasted till Seebach's death; we were granted many years before this occurred.

Conscious of facing a more vexatious dilemma than the first time, I returned to Stuttgart after the second concert and the conversation with the Count that followed it. I was aware of what I stood to lose in leaving Stuttgart. If nevertheless I finally decided for Dresden it was less the ambition of a thirty-two-year-old-man which was the cause than the musician's wish to play—instead of as up to now on a good Tyrolese fiddle—on a Stradivarius.

A whole night long I talked it over with my friend Ministerialrat[1] Frey, who cared as much for my personal well-being as for that of the State Theatre of his dear Stuttgart which had now been placed under him. We found no way out. Both of us were heavy-hearted when finally, towards morning, he got up and sadly quoted: "Go thither. I cannot keep thee back."[2]

My departure for Dresden at the end of the 1922 season was thereupon decided, and this decision filled me at the same time with very pleasant anticipations and a curious sense of depression which I could not get over. About this time I received an anonymous letter which did not conduce towards removing my depression. It came, no doubt, from someone who was well acquainted with the conditions of musical life in Saxony and gave me a serious warning not to go to Dresden. The writer brought many proofs from the long history of music in this town to show that every conductor of the Dresden Opera had had to fight against ingratitude, injustice and even persecution. He reminded me ominously of Richard Wagner's experiences in Dresden. This disquieting document coincided strangely with my own secret anxiety.

A short time after my call to Dresden, Nikisch fell ill and died, leaving a gap which could not be filled in the musical life of Germany. Several times I have taken Nikisch's place as conductor at the Gewandhaus in Leipzig, in that classic nursery of noble music of which Germany could well be proud, until the memorial to Felix Mendelssohn and the spirit of German culture were removed from thence.

As a Farewell Performance I conducted *Die Fledermaus*, which had been newly rehearsed. This displeased a section of the Swabian press, which informed me they could not have

[1] Councillor of a Government Department.
[2] Zieh hin, ich kann dich nicht halten. Wagner. *Siegfried*, Act III.

136

believed I was capable of making my farewell to Stuttgart with an operetta! The writer of these lines did not understand either that *Die Fledermaus* is a masterpiece of art or that in the midst of this cheerful music I was sad at heart. We found it hard to say good-bye to Stuttgart.

In the following years I have often been back and have always experienced the same joy which I felt so keenly from the first day I was there. To-day, on another continent, in view of the horrible destruction of this beautiful, enchanting town, I remember a day in Stuttgart in the early spring of 1918. One sunny Sunday morning, when during the night we had had many air attack alerts, there was a sudden violent explosion like thunder in the sky, followed by a long-drawn-out crash and sound of collapsing buildings. Not far from us in Heusteig-strasse an air attack had destroyed some houses under which some people were buried. Since then thirty-three years have gone by which should have meant a progress in civilisation or more than a quarter of a century. Instead of that, after a short period of development Germany has been thrown back for hundreds of years. Under the ruins there also lies buried what we young people of similar outlook each in his own modest way for a short time worked and hoped for in Stuttgart.

Chapter Eight

DRESDEN BEGINNINGS

To please the good old public I've elected
And open-eyed the people sit and wait.
A rare dramatic treat is now expected:
They take for granted it is something great.

GOETHE. FAUST I
PRELUDE IN THE THEATRE
TRANS. PHILIP WADE

FROM cheerful, comfortable Stuttgart, nestling in hills and woods, which in spite of its size and its industrial and architectural importance still retained the character of a pleasant old Swabian country town, we removed to the far more magnificent Dresden. In place of the comfortable timber buildings there was the renowned Dresden sandstone baroque; in place of the friendly middle-class atmosphere the ceremonial dignity of a town with a court. A certain empty society life was still the characteristic of many circles, though it is true they had been robbed of their court centre. On the other hand there certainly was a very good intelligent middle class.

The lower middle class represented the best Saxon type; among them were those of the teaching profession with whom a pronounced enthusiasm for music and a genuine idealism were in the blood. But unfortunately we became acquainted with other characteristics which in general differentiate the Saxons from the people of Berlin, Schleswig, Swabia and the Rhineland. We noticed a widespread propensity towards envy and slandering their neighbours, united to an inclination to jealousy which arose from an unfulfilled desire to be a somebody. These characteristics are quite foreign to me personally. I hardly realised them, and despised them if I became aware of them, whereas I should have observed them carefully.

At the time of our removal to Dresden inflation was at its height. My yearly income was at first two hundred thousand marks, and how much that really was nobody knew. It was inflation money and its value diminished every day, so that my salary in the course of the next months ran into millions and billions. It is obvious that at first the results of this depreciation of money terribly increased the difficulties of my artistic work, as the similar critical situation of the post-war period had done at Stuttgart. Even the less important singers were continually trying to get leave of absence and procure posts as guest artists in neighbouring Czechoslovakia. The salaries they got there supported them and their families for many weeks much better than would have been possible with a whole year's salary in Germany.

As up to now I had only conducted two concerts in Dresden as a guest conductor, the working of the Opera there was unknown to me except for the world-wide fame that the establishment enjoyed, and those artists who were of international rank. The greater number of the singers were strangers to me. Beethoven's *Fidelio* was chosen for the opening performance. While I was still on my summer holiday I received a telegram from the manager with the following laconic question: "Who shall sing the first Leonora?"

Five interpreters of this ticklish part were at our disposal in the rich personnel of the Dresden singers. Each of them had *one* of the many necessary qualifications for the part, a perfect performance of which will hardly ever be seen. In the first of the ladies, who bore a celebrated name, the Opera possessed an artist of feeling and imagination who had much impressed me. Unfortunately she was no longer as young as she had been and her vocal imperfections were such that you could think yourself lucky if she did not sing more than a semi-tone flat. Another singer had a beautiful voice but an impossible figure; the third a blameless figure but not much of a voice. The fourth, who was satisfactory as regards voice *and* figure, was so shortsighted that without thick eyeglasses she could make no contact with the conductor. The fifth, a young singer, united a beautiful voice with all the other requirements but had no singing technique or experience whatever. She had been engaged only as a hope for the future. And there the matter ended.

From a distance it was impossible to come to a decision as to this important selection. At first I remained silent. Only after a repeated urgent demand I telegraphed back crossly: "The eldest." I thus had peace until my arrival in Dresden when, after considering the relative values of the singers, I could appoint the first Leonora.

The rehearsal of *Fidelio* and, in addition, *Rosenkavalier* and *Die Meistersinger*, had not been going on for a week when a pressing telephone call from the Reichs Chancellery summoned me to conduct the Philharmonic Orchestra in Berlin at the first celebration of the foundation of the German Republic. The concert was to take place on the following day—a Friday. It was the personal wish of President Ebert that I should be in charge of the musical part of the festival.

The Secretary of State, who was at the telephone, did not admit the validity of my refusal on the grounds that it was impossible for me to go away in the middle of the *Fidelio* rehearsals and before my first opera performance in Dresden.

He observed crossly: "If His Majesty the Emperor of Germany had commanded you to come you would already have been sitting in the train. You think you can refuse the wishes of the President."

"You're quite wrong," I called back in a rage. "All right, I'll come. But I have *Fidelio* here on Sunday. I must rehearse it on Saturday morning."

"Of course, Herr Generalmusikdirektor. The night train ..."

"Quite impossible. I could not catch it after the performance. You must arrange for a car to take me to Dresden."

"With pleasure."

At the Anhalter station an official from the Chancellery received me with a surprised look at the red necktie which I had put on quite unintentionally. It was clear that this colour would have irritated him less in conjunction with black and white.[1]

The festival of the constitution, at which Gerhart Hauptmann was present as a guest of honour in the President's box, took place, and when it was over it appeared that the car for my return journey had been completely forgotten. The friendly chief of police, Richter, with some difficulty finally succeeded in procuring an open taxi, in which I went off just as I was, in my tail coat. I soon saw that the worthy chauffeur could not find his way anywhere except in Berlin. As I could not help him I simply went to sleep. When I woke up I realised that we were approaching Dessau, a town which was certainly not expecting me for a dress rehearsal of *Fidelio*. When we finally did reach Dresden next day, I was obliged, in order to be in time, to begin the rehearsal in my tail coat at ten in the morning.

A short time before I had been appointed, Dr. Alfred Reucker from Zürich had been appointed as Generalintendant of the Dresden State Theatre. I worked with him for eleven years until we left together in 1933. Reucker brought to the much sought after position in Dresden, to which he had been appointed chiefly through Seebach's recommendation, all the comprehensive knowledge and experience that could be wished for. Stage-struck at sixteen, he had joined a touring company and soon found work in small theatres; later he worked at Prague with Angelo Neumann, from whom he learnt a great deal. After that he had been Intendant at Zürich for about twenty years. Modest and unpretentious, he thought only of doing his duty and into this he put all his unusual talents.

In physical size he was as big as Seebach. He was more practical, less emotional, than the latter and sometimes lacked a certain boldness which is desirable in theatrical management.

---

[1] Black, white and red were the colours of Imperial Germany, abandoned by the Reich in 1918, red the colour of the extreme left.

He was, however, reliability itself. His memory for the least detail of whatever he had undertaken was unbelievable. Once I said to him bitterly that it was impossible for me to go on working with a certain technically incapable employee. Reucker, who thought I was right, said it would be very difficult to dismiss an official who had been engaged for life. In spite of that he would make the attempt but it might take two years. So I had to carry on fretful and annoyed. However, two years later Reucker came into my room and said: "There, we have got rid of X."

What he had undertaken he carried through with determination. That we did not always agree is to be easily understood from the difference of our characters. If I was too impetuous for Reucker he used to quote: "If I deliberated I should not be Tell."[1] The twenty-two years between us made it impossible for me to harangue him in my usual way.

His habitual expression, "It looks black to me", became a household word in the theatre and the family circle.

Reucker's character and disposition reminded one in many ways of Brüning, the Reich's Chancellor, whom I later got to know in England, in his moral sobriety and the painful exactitude with which he administered the money entrusted to him: in particular the public money to which he was himself entitled for his official business. On the innumerable journeys which he undertook in the interests of the Dresden State Theatre, a second-class ticket on the railway and rooms at the best hotel would have been allowed without any objection. He, however, travelled third class on principle and lived modestly. When he took a taxi, if he could not avoid this expenditure, he never used it beyond what was indispensable for his official object or he would have conscientiously paid back the difference in price from his own pocket.

He watched with self-sacrifice over the observance of the orders for measures of state economy. He kept his own hands clean from the injustice of laying more burdens, however in-

[1] *Wilhelm Tell*. Schiller.

142

significant, on the struggling state. One can imagine the disgust with which at this time of need he learnt of arrogant foreign artists who lived as guests of the State Opera at the Hotel Belle-vue and wished to have their breakfast champagne put down to the account of the State of Saxony. Such excesses Reucker failed completely to understand and his wounded sense of decency sometimes drove this dignified man to extremes of vehemence and a stiff, unbending attitude.

Unfortunately, Reucker's great experience and knowledge of men did not prevent me from committing one of the most stupid acts of my life. When he came to Stuttgart in 1922 to discuss my contract with me, I asked for and received from the Saxon government through him the same appointment for life as had been given, amongst other things, to Richard Wagner. Without being aware of it, I acted for exactly the same reasons as he had: the permanency of the Opera Director's position would give him more authority with the artists.

How far the hopes of my great predecessor were fulfilled in this respect those who are interested may read in Wagner's autobiography *Mein Leben*. In any case my pretensions brought me out of the frying pan into the fire. As a government official, all my conduct was now treated with a publicity com-pletely different from what it would have been in the case of an appointment by private contract. The seeds of many per-verted criticisms germinated and in time put forth the most luxuriant bloom. The gloomy harvest that I reaped was envy and hatred.

When I took up my appointment every misgiving was for-gotten, everyone's happiness, mine as well as others', was with-out a shadow. Fate had placed me in Dresden in a situation in which all the essentials—nature, art and good traditions—were united as is seldom the case. The outward appearance of the Opera House itself raised the highest expectations. The building, Semper's work, was a jewel of beauty. The general aspect of the town which it dominated, together with the Hofkirche so imaginatively designed, the Zwinger, the Elbe and the Brühlshe

Terrace in the near distance, was unparalleled. The interior of
the Opera House was of the same unusual quality: alike the
splendid auditorium and the wide compass of the stage which
possessed every imaginable technical device and an unequalled
complete theatrical equipment.

The framework was here on which, after overcoming difficulties due to the unsettled times which might be only temporary, the Dresden Opera could be built up again in all its
former splendour. The worthy state orchestra remained unimpaired; its unity, virtuosity and magnificent tone had carried
me away at the first hearing. My care would have to be devoted
to the far more difficult, sensitive and unstable condition of the
singers which, owing to the hard times and the interregnum,
appeared like a neglected garden. But even in this assemblage
of unequal value there was a set of unique performers whose
quality showed the superiority of the Dresden Opera over most
other German theatres. If one could unite these artists in one
cast, performances would materialise which would give a fresh
spur to my faith in the possibility of ideal performances of
opera. I was determined with all my youthful strength to
extract the best possible production from the actual conditions.

Enthusiasm reigned everywhere, the press was enraptured
with the new man from whom wonders were expected.
"Habemus Papam," wrote the critic of an important newspaper
on the right. Those on the left compared me to King Midas,
who changed everything he touched into gold.

It was obvious that this paroxysm could not last. The critic
who was well versed in the classics appeared with a parcel of
symphonies which my performance was to "change into
gold". The other gentleman wished above all for sacrificial
ceremonies for his god Richard Wagner, and when these had
been celebrated the Pope should not forget the creations of his
son Siegfried. Later he declared it was superfluous to take a
"meaningless piece of bungling" like Berlioz's *Benvenuto
Cellini* into the repertory, and swore he would not hear the
work again "until Siegfried Wagner's *Bärenhäuter* or *Herzog*

Wildfang should have obtained from the Musikdirektor the attention that was their due."

After the persistent attempts of a third writer to bring out his wretched little daughter as the first soubrette at the opera had miscarried, the critical papa in future regretted the opera director's lack of understanding of beautiful voices and the *bel canto* style.

Much less of a problem than the opera—actually too little of a problem—were the twelve yearly symphony concerts. With the rare exceptions of guest performances by Richard Strauss, Siegmund von Hausegger, Otto Klemperer, they were by tradition exclusively under the direction of the generalmusikdirektor. The taste of the concert audience was entirely conservative. The trouble I was always taking to make the Dresden musicians and music lovers acquainted with valuable contemporary works came up against a complete and chilly rejection. They wanted to hear the classics and romantics, of which they were never weary. A certain self-satisfied boredom differentiated this public clearly from that of Stuttgart, which allowed itself to be surprised time after time. The best thing, the often magnificent performances of the orchestra which could not fail to delight a musician, was considered so much a matter of course that after the sensation of my first concerts only a few of my listeners still went to the expense of going into an ecstasy.

According to custom, in the Dresden concerts the chief emphasis was on the orchestra and conductor. This was in contrast to the neighbouring Leipzig Gewandhaus, at whose performances solo players were regularly engaged. At Dresden there appeared now and then at these evenings only internationally known pianists like Schnabel, Sauer, Egon Petri, violinists like Hubermann, Szigeti, Franz von Vecsey who died young, and my brother.

It was a great pleasure to me to meet Rudolf Serkin, the eighteen-year-old pianist, at his frequent appearances. Adolf had brought him to Stuttgart when hardly more than a child, not long previously. In Dresden his rendering, especially of the

145

Fifth Brandenburg Concerto, excited unusual enthusiasm immediately after the cadenza at the end of the first movement, which he played with unheard-of power and intensity of expression. It was not difficult to foresee Serkin's great future, even then.

Whether my brother had become dissatisfied once again with his pianist or whether the latter had fallen ill, Adolf found himself at Vienna looking for a substitute when friends drew his attention to the young, highly gifted Serkin, a pupil of the piano teacher Robert. They went to his house to find him. To the horror of the emissary it appeared that Rudi, at that very moment, was on the way to France with a group of other underfed children sent by a welfare society to convalesce. Adolf's friend practically pulled him out of the train, a slender, serious, shy fifteen-year-old boy with untidy black hair and intelligent eyes. Two musicians who as men and artists were to understand each other's talents peculiarly well came together at that moment in a lasting collaboration. If the train at the Vienna West station had whistled away on its journey earlier they would perhaps have passed each other by.

The splendid Dresden symphony concerts remained for the greater part of the public a pleasant addition to the winter musical life; with the possibilities of playing a part in building up social life, as Paul Bekker said. Dresden was and remained a town of the theatre, or rather of the opera.

I worked diligently in common with Reucker chiefly to introduce permanently into the programme important works that were not known or seldom performed in Dresden. Amongst these was Verdi's *Othello*, which had not been heard for many years and was given with a novel kind of production. On this Verdi evening the beginnings of a style of production appeared which were afterwards fully developed in Berlin in *Un Ballo in Maschera*. In the meantime the chief difference between my early experience with opera in Dresden and all that I had had before lay in the incomparable magnificence now given by the quality of sound in the orchestra.

Othello was followed by Pfitzner's *Palestrina* in the presence of the composer, who had not altered in any particular since Stuttgart. Only his usual bad temper was increased by his bodily ill-health. In order to cheer him up the composer was taken to an excellent restaurant. The peevish fellow was in no way averse from a well-furnished table and a bottle of red wine but he kept the waiter on the run for half an hour. In vain he consulted himself and us as to what he should order. He had a great longing for a chop cooked in cream but, thinking of his biliousness, he countermanded it. Fish was ordered and likewise sent away again. Finally he decided crossly he would have something quite insipid, very light. He had hardly eaten it when he turned as white as chalk and hurried away. After a long absence he returned, letting himself fall exhausted into his seat with the languid announcement that he had not been able to retain even the "very light" dish. A glance withered the logician of the party, who observed: "Then, master, you might just as well have eaten the chop cooked in cream."

Pfitzner's artistic opposite, Feruccio Busoni, was at that time a very sick man whom unfortunately I had got to know and respect too late. I was happy to give his one-act opera *Arlecchino* its first appearance at Dresden. Busoni died before we gave the première of his last, most significant work, *Doktor Faust*.

The most important operatic event of the first Dresden winter season 1922–23 was Moussorgski's *Boris Godunow*. At Stuttgart I had already reached the conclusion that the expressionistic staging we had used there had been a mistake because of the historical subject-matter. For some time Dresden had been under the aegis of the Russian refugee movement and was strongly influenced by the force of the Asiatic spirit which, owing to this cause, disclosed itself to Western Europe in many stirring details. A writer who was much read at the time closed a volume of essays on contemporary problems with a short survey of the "light from the East". He there threw out the question: Could it be conceivable that in the future history of man the power of love and sympathy could take the place of the sword? A beautiful Utopia—the astonishing Russians them-selves have not done least to make a *reductio ad absurdum* of it.

By dint of searching around and following many different tracks, I succeeded in finding the producer to suit me in a Russian musician who came to my room at the Opera one day to ask for a free seat. In answer to my questions he revealed himself, after a short conversation, as a kapellmeister who had conducted *Boris Godunow* much oftener than I had, and of course in Russia itself. With the skill in acting of his race he immediately interpreted the coronation scene to me. The small, miserable, emaciated creature threw himself down in my room, touched the floor with his forehead, and seemed as if he never wanted to get up. The score indicates after the pealing of the Kremlin bells a long pause, which I at the piano wished to pass over lightly without attributing to it any special meaning. When my Russian still did not move from the floor I asked with astonishment what was the meaning of his behaviour. With much emotion he told me that during this pause in the music, in which the crowd remained in complete silence, Chaliapine, the great performer of Tsar Boris, used to kiss the Russian earth with solemn fervour.

From this example I realised how impossible it would be for a German producer to make contact with this opera. To Reucker's horror and against his violent opposition, I carried through on the spot the appointment of my strange visitor as producer of *Boris Godunow*. His peculiar aptitude for this job was obvious. Reucker foresaw plainly the disorder that the character of this highly gifted intruder must introduce later on into the quiet progress of work in the opera. I lived in the moment and was on fire to collaborate with the Russian. Chudjakoff, a highly imaginative scene-painter, also a Russian, was snatched away from the cabaret *Der Blaue Vogel* in Berlin by Reucker. He was to supply us with the scenery for *Boris Godunow* and for that purpose came temporarily to Dresden.

Chudjakoff's Asiatic temperament made it difficult to excite him to persist in his work. After delivering the very beautiful sketches of scenery up to the scene of the Kremlin he suddenly vanished and returned to Berlin. Reucker caught him again and the work began anew. But one Saturday, very early in the morning, the watchman came to my room in the Dresden Opera House and begged me to go to the canteen. "Something queer is up, sir."[1]

I found the respectable room, devoted to sausage and light ale, swimming in champagne. Scene-shifters, cleaning women, firemen, all with glasses in their hands, were in a more than dubious condition. Chudjakoff, the host, was sitting on a table and, with genuine Russian catholicity of feeling, embracing and kissing the dear men and the dear women indiscriminately, alternately crying and laughing and inviting "little father, little pigeon"—that was myself—to a share in the feast. Champagne was literally flowing in streams. Unfortunately I had to put an end to the jollification and have Chudjakoff carried off to bed.

Shortly afterwards I got out of him that he had signed a splendid contract to go to the United States and had immediately spent part of the advance on his salary in dollars, so almighty in 1922, in providing this feast for the *tovarishs*.

A few days later he wished to take ship at Bremen. He had lost all interest in *Boris*—he "wasn't thinking about it any more".

As I had to have my last designs I dragged him unwillingly into the store of the Opera where everything necessary for him to complete his work had been prepared, including strong coffee and cigarettes. To his no small astonishment I locked him in.

Next morning, when I let him out, I received everything my heart could desire, down to the last sketch, without the good-natured son of the steppes bearing me any grudge for having robbed him of his freedom. When he left he forgot to collect his fee, which the Dresden Opera owes him to this day.

[1] "Da wärnse was erlähm, Herr Generalmusikdirekter!"

This highly gifted work obtained an unusual success. With it *Boris Godunow* became part of the German opera repertory.

Foreign countries also took notice of this resuscitation, and the Dresden Opera Company was the first German theatrical enterprise to take part in the International Zürich Festival of 1923 with a performance of *Boris*. This guest performance was followed by others in the same town, as well as at the League of Nations meetings in Geneva.

In Dresden the theatre was full of life—this was the universal opinion, over and over again confirmed with vigour by the foreign press as well. We brought forward many works by young composers. On the occasion of *Arlecchino*, Busoni had recommended his pupil Kurt Weill to me. His short opera *Der Protagonist* received its first performance at Dresden. With Weill were associated Krenek, Hindemith, Brand and others.

The most pressing problem, even more important for the normal management of the Opera, how to achieve a thorough overhauling of the current classical repertory, was harder to solve. For the time being I had to put up in silence with the reproach that a regrettable defect in the new director was his obvious lack of a love for Mozart. However, the fundamental reason why Mozart's works seldom appeared in the programme was not taken into account. It lay in the insufficiency of the solo ensemble which, naturally enough, comprised a set of distinguished opera performers but did not dispose of enough young, beautiful voices for the performance of Mozart's works. It was the same with other theatres, which were mostly worse off than we were.

We therefore betook ourselves to the search for young talent, with varying success but doubtless causing much bad humour among the "old guard" of the singers.

In the cause of art I disregarded many feelings, natural to humanity but not to the purpose. I myself had no feeling for prestige or personal sensibility, nor could I understand such things in others, and consequently did not spare them. I was not naturally given to grumbling or fault-finding; rather the opposite. Only I was "every moment dissatisfied"[1] because I was looking for perfection and seldom found it.

The door of the Dresden Opera House was open to everyone who believed he had talent. In the first years I was so full of the belief that I should make a wonderful discovery in this sphere that I arranged daily auditions on the stage, and in the course of time personally tested thousands of singers. I did not find much that was really useful. Yet I had the sad satisfaction, on the other hand, of finding that none of the candidates I turned away in the search for greatness ever came to anything noteworthy elsewhere. One must come to terms with the fact that a singer who approaches the ideal to any extent is an extraordinarily rare phenomenon.

At the moment at which the difficulties in Dresden were piling up, both in the solution of artistic problems and in the internal management, I was lucky enough in 1925 to find a colleague who afforded me the most essential assistance. Erich Engel had been the musical assistant of Leo Blech, Bruno Walter, and other conductors, at the Charlottenburg Opera. He had earned an unusual fame in the German world of opera, far beyond the boundaries of where he worked, by productions of such quality as, though quietly achieved, seldom remain unknown. By renouncing for himself the career of kapellmeister—an unusual man in an unusual position—he used his wide knowledge to develop his sphere of action in a way which his title—"leader of musical studies"—did not explain, hardly even hinted at.

Until we left Dresden together, and during our long collaboration at the Colon Theatre in Buenos Aires, he carried out his work in an inimitable fashion. His culture, his knowledge and incorruptible impartiality, united to the most tenacious zeal for work that can be imagined, made Engel a unique figure.

In the true sense of the words "a good angel",[2] he now took

[1] "unbefriedigt jeden Augenblick."
[2] Engel: German for angel.

into his own hands all the business which up to now had diverted me from my own work. He took charge of the continuous auditions, the meagre results of which bore no relation to the time I had spent on them away from my proper occupations. From now on, he and the two other Kapellmeisters separated the chaff from the wheat and only brought those of real talent for me to judge. Besides this, a fee of ten marks in aid of charity was now to be paid for each audition. This would reduce the number of tests we were quite willing to make, within bearable limits.

One day Kapellmeister Kutzschbach came to my room just as I was going home after a fatiguing rehearsal of *Tristan*. In his Saxon dialect he said: "I have already executed twenty, sir. They were no good. But one of them is carrying on terribly and says he only paid the ten marks because he wanted to sing to the Musikdirektor in person. Do us the kindness of hearing the man so that we don't get into trouble. No one knows what the chap is capable of; his singing is horrible."[1]

I went into the stalls which, in spite of the unusual hour—three in the afternoon—were thronged with curious people; in the theatre it soon gets about that "something is up".

A miserable, small fellow came gaily on to the stage and to my question what he was going to sing answered: "Obs du mich liebst." This is a composition of Lincke's which he "could sing by heart".[2]

After two minutes he was dispatched off the stage down to my room, where I said one or two friendly things about his shameless behaviour. He replied, smiling: "Don't get angry, sir. Look here, I've got a job in a soap factory at Pirna; well,

---

[1] Herr Generalmusikdirekter, mr ham wieder zwanz'sch geschlachded. 'swar nischt dabei. Aber eener doobt firchterlich und sacht, er hat die zähn Mark blos bezahld, weiler 'm Generalmusikdirekter berseenlich vorsing 'n will. Tunse uns den Gefallen un hähr 'n sich den Mann an, damid mr keene Schwierigkeiden kriechen. Niemand weess, wozu so 'n Kerl fä'ch is; sing' n dud 'r scheisslich.

[2] Aus 'n Koppe kenne.

and so the boss said, 'If *you* get an audition from the Musik-direktor in person then *I* will pay the ten marks.' Well, so I had to do something about it!"[1]

And with a sly grin he added: "And besides that, I never go out without taking a little box of our soap with me; well, and so when I had sung, the court singers laughed terribly and what d'you think Herr Director—then I sold them twenty-four marks worth of soap!"[2]

It was not always easy to keep one's patience and control one's nerves when every day, in spite of a staff of many excellent colleagues, one had to worry over the trifles of the many-sided opera business. The situation of the leading German opera houses such as Berlin, Dresden, Vienna, Munich, was then becoming more and more difficult. One of the reasons was that the munificence and expenditure on scenery of the reigning houses no longer came to their support. Even if the unavoidable deficit had been made up by subsidies on a large scale from the state or the town there was no compensation for the incentive of titles and orders which, strangely enough, had previously decided many singers in negotiating a contract. The competition in appointing artists of merit just now, when economy was the most pressing law of the government, only resulted in a general auction which in consequence soon made salaries rise to incredible heights.

In the end, the steady-going Reucker succeeded, through the Union of German Theatre Managers, in laying down a fee of a thousand marks in stabilised currency as the extreme limit for one appearance of singers who were much in demand. Frauds and profiteering were, however, not stopped. In Berlin

---

[1] Rächn 'se sich ne uff, Herr Generalmusikdirekter. Sähnsemal, ich bin nämlich inn 'r Seefenfabrik in Pirne angestellt; na un nu had meen Meester gesacht 'Wenn *Du* 'n Generalmusikdirekter perseenlich vorsingst, da zahl *ich* de zähn Mark.' Nu da musst 'chse doch selber bemieh'n!"

[2] "Ausserdäm gäh' ch doch aber nie aus, ohne'n Kefferchen mit unsrer Seefe beim 'r zu fiehren; nu, un wie 'ch nu gesung hab, da ha 'm die Gammersänger firchterlich gelacht, un was gloo 'mse, Herr Generalmusik-direkter; da hab ich 'n doch noch fier zwanz'ch Mark Seefe verkoofd!"

alone the series of privately organised concerts that sprang up like rank weeds made our lives difficult. It was characteristic that in a new production of *Die Fledermaus* we could get a particularly charming Rosalinde only because we raised no objection to her appearing at the same time, so to speak, in Berlin. She there took the part in Revue which, I am sorry to say, the great Max Reinhardt made out of *Die Fledermaus*, though it was certainly successful—while with us it was given in original classical form.

To mention another embarrassment of a theatre director: he who pays the piper calls the tune. Whether earlier, during the time of royal patronage, this had been a pleasant or painful by-product, the interference of diverse individuals welded together in one body such as a Landtag[1] or town council, proved now to be a far worse evil.

Count Seebach was not only the first but perhaps the only one in Dresden to realise quickly how thankless the work of managing a big opera was in these post-war days. His sense of justice had always caused him to intervene on behalf of Reucker and me when stupidity or malevolence displayed itself against us. Occasionally he remarked thoughtfully: "It should not always be forgotten that I used to have a king at my back."

In spite of all, I felt unreserved admiration for the way in which government and town, in the hardest of times, took it for granted that they must support the theatre without a penny coming in from private sources. Originally owing their existence to the love or caprice of individual princes, in 1918 the theatres and the far more costly operas had become the property of the people, who were conscious of their responsibility for this inheritance—and this was one of the few points on which the young republic was unanimous. This was not only the case for the few well-known theatres. In a similar spirit seventy to eighty of the smaller towns prided themselves on the continued existence of their theatres in spite of the

[1] Provincial legislative assembly.

154

greatest distress, so that one of the finest branches of German civilisation should not wither.

Even to-day in the ruin of Germany the same thing has happened again in all the zones.

In the years of my emigration, when I saw foreign theatres at the service of business or light amusement—not always but very often—I realised fully by comparison how much the Weimar Republic was to be thanked for holding fast and loyally to Schiller's idea of the theatre as "a moral institution".

Riots and street fighting, which we had experienced under the Spartacus rule at the beginning of 1919 in Berlin, and in the following spring in Stuttgart, did not cease till towards the end of 1923. Up to this time the atmosphere of inflation made life and art more difficult and damped our happiness, though sometimes, by the loosening of restraint, the bonds of an out-of-date tradition were undone, and gave room to the creative activity of young and new people. Social, material and political misery harassed everyone without exception. The conditions of the day with their many varied currents—in the German Reichstag there were members of twenty-four parties!—created a suitable ground on which every passing chatterbox, every private scribbler pursuing his personal interests, could unload his refuse.

A mass meeting which was to take place in the big Opera Square would have interfered with the evening performance. The deputation sent to me to arrange the meeting allowed common sense to bring it to reason. Such distressed conditions in the country were certainly no matter for rejoicing.

In the summer of 1925 the Saxon government resolved to institute a representative demonstration in honour of the German Reich's constitution with which the Weimar Republic had stabilised itself. The sense of these celebrations could really only be to emphasise the uniting force of the democratic government as opposed to the diversity of the various districts and parties. The highly industrialised Saxony had at that time a large left wing majority in the government.

A telegram surprised me by calling me back from my summer holidays to undertake the musical direction of this national celebration in Dresden. The programme was to include the *Egmont* Overture and Beethoven's Fifth Symphony. I was told that Thomas Mann would speak on the character and aims of the Weimar constitution.

For many years I had been not only a convinced admirer of this great writer but I felt myself intellectually in agreement with him in his outlook on politics and art. Many personal meetings had confirmed my belief in the conformity of our ideas. Among his essays I, as a musician, was especially pleased with the courageous stand he took as to the problem of Richard Wagner's life and work, which he treated without reserve with superior technical knowledge and with profound affection for the man of genius.

My disappointment was great when, on arriving in Dresden, I found that not Thomas Mann but another writer was to speak, one who, apart from his literary insignificance, was alien to me owing to his radical politics.

The members of the State Orchestra as well as myself had been hastily recalled from their holidays, but the arrangements turned out to have been precipitately improvised. Labour unrest and inflation had reached their highest point, feelings were gloomy and depressed. Nervous tension weighed noticeably on the Dresden Opera House, where all the seats were taken— the stalls and balconies by state officials and professors from the various Saxon universities and schools—a public that represented the élite of Saxony's intellectual life.

After a listless performance of the *Egmont* Overture a deathly silence reigned, as if even this music had no power to stimulate or arouse any feeling. Then the curtain went up and the speaker turned to the meeting and made a demagogic address full of violent insults *against* the government.

It was an unfortunate speech. It would have been in place at a communist meeting: here the government, struggling with difficulty for union, was stabbed in the back.

156

When the lecturer called the Chancellor Cuno a "living corpse" I expected that a storm of indignation would break out in the auditorium. All these men, representatives of the country's educated officials, had taken an oath to support the Weimar constitution just as I had; they had eaten the bread of the Republic, however meagre it might be in spite of the "billions".

Nothing happened. Only in the dress circle a door slammed and I heard Graf Seebach leave the hall saying audibly, "Filth!"[1]

I felt as he did. While I still stood petrified at my desk my indignation at the disgraceful situation began to grow. Quite incapable of pulling myself together, I began the Fifth Symphony. After the first movement I threw the stick away and went out. How could I conduct music—especially the triumphant last movement of the Fifth—when thousands of so-called educated men allowed uncontradicted abuse of a government we had assembled to celebrate!

The meeting broke up when I did not come back. I expected my dismissal next day, or at least disciplinary action. But once more nothing happened.

A few months later Hitler made his Munich *putsch* and with that, in this unlucky year, the general public became aware of his existence for the first time. At that moment the world was still able, by the temporary removal of its originator, to ward off the evil that menaced it.

[1] Schweinerei.

Chapter Nine

AN INTERMEZZO

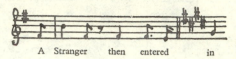

RICHARD WAGNER
DIE WALKURE. ACT I

"Dear Sir,

"Even before the death of Hans Richter, Frau Cosima had entrusted me with the organisation of the orchestra for the Bayreuth Festival. So far I have heard no complaints that I carried out this work inefficiently. I am therefore not in need of your support. On the other hand, I wish to take this opportunity of saying that, as far as the pleasure of a personal acquaintance is concerned, to which you refer in your letter, I for my part am by no means certain that I ought to attach importance to it. I am told that you are a good conductor of the works of Reger and Brahms, two composers whom I highly esteem. Whether you are, in addition, in a position to do justice to Wagner's complete artistic works, in Bayreuth, still remains to be proved.

"Your obedient servant,
"Dr. Karl Muck."

I received this letter at the beginning of the year 1924, after Siegfried Wagner had handed over to me the reopening of Bayreuth with *Die Meistersinger* after an interval of ten years. As I was not acquainted with Muck's peculiarities I had offered my help in collecting an orchestra to my elderly colleague, who had returned to Germany a few years earlier after a long absence in America. I thought that by this I could do a service to Bayreuth because, owing to my many travels in Germany as a guest conductor, I had systematically impressed on my mind a knowledge of the orchestras' new blood, which was unknown to Muck.

158

So there I was, already at the start with a nasty knock in the eye!

The invitation to conduct at Bayreuth, apart from the compliment it conveyed, had fulfilled one of my dearest wishes—to be in that place where there must be the greatest artistic possibilities of developing all Wagner's ideas.

On a beautiful June day, at about five in the morning, I arrived at Bayreuth. I hurried away from the station to the hill where the Festival theatre stands.

In the woods behind the simple tile-roofed building, where, at this early hour of the morning the deepest peace reigned, I lay down in the grass, and in spite of the dignity of my position in Dresden, behaved like a genuine German Michael.[1] I rejoiced at the thought of the work, than which I could imagine nothing better. I swore to myself, very seriously, to do my part with all my might; in short, I was altogether in the enthusiastic condition of a musician who finds himself face to face with a new problem.

At about eight o'clock there was a sound of choral singing. In a primitive wooden shed Professor Hugo Rüdel, the master of the Berlin Cathedral Choir and of the State Opera Chorus, was rehearsing *Die Meistersinger*.

The choristers had been selected from different German theatres, so that not only their vocal quality but their appearance could be taken into consideration.

What I was now listening to might be the second or third choral rehearsal. Why should I not at once take part in it? I rose from the grass and entered the shed.

Rüdel and I did not know each other, although of course I knew he was a first-class musician and chorus master. Through a window I saw the stout man with his scanty moustache standing in front of a grand piano and rehearsing the scene of the riot with great vehemence. Going up to him I asked: "May I introduce myself? My name is Busch. I have come . . ."

[1] The typical German countryman—honest, long-suffering, but slow.

159

Rüdel, buried in what he was doing, interrupted me brusquely. "Go and stand with the tenors!"

"Excuse me for interrupting," I said, "I have come . . ."

I did not reach the end of my sentence "to conduct *Die Meistersinger*" for he cried out: "Good God! Go to the second tenors! I have already waited for you all day!"

I went to the second tenors. I could not disturb the passionate man any longer. A singer gave me his part and kindly showed me the place where they were rehearsing.

After some time, during which I sang heartily with the others, Rüdel suddenly slammed down the lid of the piano, took a deep breath and exclaimed excitedly (it was said he used to begin the day with a half-bottle of Burgundy instead of a cup of coffee, but this may easily have been an exaggeration): "Gentlemen, this won't do! I should not dare to present a chorus like this to the Musikdirektor Busch when he comes here for the first time. I don't know the gentleman, but they say he is very exacting. If he hears you all croaking like that he will immediately go away again. We must try it separately. Tenors alone!"

So, among the fifty sons of Anak, I sang my part till the interval. Then I told Rüdel—this time without letting him interrupt—that I was Busch, the Musikdirektor, and had come to conduct *Die Meistersinger*.

The old man turned pale. For him, who had spent most of his life at the Berlin court opera, titles still meant something. I had to remove his embarrassment, stop his excuses as regards the chorus, which was still standing round, and try to win his confidence. I invited him to lunch at my hotel, *Zur Post*, and had a bottle of his favourite Rhine wine put on ice.

At one o'clock, midday, we met for lunch and I should be suspected of exaggeration if I said at what hour we parted. At any rate, only one waiter was at hand, who had to be woken by us from his weary slumbers when the light of morning shone into the garden.

Rüdel and I had become friends. During those hours I heard

many of his interesting reminiscences. Above all, he told me of his experiences with Hans Richter and other great masters in Bayreuth and Berlin. He promised me that when he had finished studying the scene of the riot the chorus would sing it unaccompanied. I bet, on the other hand, that the solo singers, who usually made a pretence of singing in this finale or did not even open their mouths, would also join in to the smallest detail and would not require instrumental support either.

"It makes a great difference whether you sing the wrong notes or the right ones!"[1] In an almost menacing voice, his watery blue eyes fixed on me, he often used to repeat this saying when blaming a singer's inaccuracy in an *ensemble* where no personal success could be achieved.

We did really both win our bets. I studied the *ensemble* of the *Meister* so thoroughly that when the soloists came to sing it with the chorus both groups were able to get through their parts without making a mistake.

I personally held about a hundred rehearsals of the individual singers for the performance of *Die Meistersinger*, for the musical assistants at my disposal were not of much use. Even more regrettable was it that, as I had feared beforehand, the quality of singers was not faultless. What was lacking in beauty of tone and vigour could only be compensated for by the greatest exactitude.

When Muck began his rehearsals of *Parsifal* I at once noticed that here, too, a great deal was not as it should have been. Inferior but ambitious performers had placed themselves in the front rows, while excellent ones remained at the back desks for the sake of peace. I consequently made quite a new distribution of the musicians for my *Meistersinger*.

After the first rehearsal which Muck had listened to, he came to me and exclaimed: "That is quite a different orchestra! You have much better wind players than I have!"

[1] Es ist ein ander Ding ob falsch man oder richtig sing. *Die Meistersinger*, Act III.

Thereupon, at the next *Parsifal* rehearsal, he claimed my first wind players as well, with the result that jealousy immediately sprang up in the orchestra. If one of the players was pleased at seeing his powers recognised by both Kapellmeisters he was at the same time annoyed at having to do double work for the same pay. Another was cross at being undeservedly put in the background. With one accord they all grumbled. A meeting of members of the orchestra was held in which, as usual, the least valuable members were victorious because they opened their mouths widest. At this meeting a vote of censure was passed against Muck and myself, which did not disturb us much.

On the other hand, an article I had written for the *Bayreuther Blätter* on the future of the Festival was the occasion of much vexation for me. The effects of the 1918 revolution, the political and social upheavals of the following years, had not yet been surmounted, and the German orchestras, formerly so justly celebrated, had not yet recovered their previous high standard. In America, besides the Boston Symphony Orchestra which, long before the war, had occupied a distinguished position, there were now a whole set of first-class orchestras, in no way inferior to the best German ones. I ventured to express these facts frankly. In particular there was *one* personality whose distinguished performance I brought to the notice of German musicians as an example—Arturo Toscanini. He had completely reorganised the Milan Scala after the war and quickly brought it back to its former eminence.

The result of my enthusiastic reference to the great Italian was that I was suspected of "lack of patriotic sentiment".

Siegfried told me that Toscanini had let him know that it was his great wish to conduct in Bayreuth. For that he was prepared for any sacrifice. I advised most urgently that the *maestro* should immediately be engaged for the 1925 season to conduct *Tristan and Isolde*. The answer I received was: "A foreigner is really not suitable for Bayreuth."

My plea led to nothing, for Siegfried Wagner could be very

obstinate. He was also afraid that Toscanini would be too un-bending in his demands, intolerant with his colleagues, in short, disturbing to the peace of the Bayreuth atmosphere. A few years later Toscanini's unbending character brought Bayreuth a fame and also a financial success that it might have had earlier.

It must unfortunately be said that when the original refusal became untenable Wahnfried rushed to the opposite extreme—a Toscanini-hysteria, which knew no bounds. One had the melancholy impression that there had never been a Hans Richter, Felix Mottl or Karl Muck in the Festival Theatre.

Meantime, after some experiences together, I was on the best footing with Muck. After the orchestra rehearsals I was able to ask him to tell me his opinion honestly, for in forming a judgment as to the tone and the balance between stage and orchestra the impression is different in the auditorium and at the conductor's desk. This is especially the case with a sunk orchestra where one is lost in the mass of sound. Muck criticised me thoroughly and sharply, although he was not lacking in appreciation.

I still remember his intelligent and correct observations with gratitude.

The opening performance of *Die Meistersinger*, prepared with love and scrupulous care, arrived at last. Everyone felt the significance of the moment when, after an interval of ten years, the curtain once again rose on the stage of Richard Wagner's theatre. No one suspected what the theatre devil secretly intended to do with this curtain in the course of the performance.

When after a beautiful and successful first act I stood at my desk and received the light signal to begin the second, the curtain went up at the appointed moment. Half a yard above the stage it stuck, and hung thoughtfully, then shamefacedly sank down again. From behind it the chorus of apprentices was heard singing "Johannistag". Then there was silence and I had to stop.

I waited for another light signal, to begin again from the beginning.

The curtain did not wait. This time, at the second bar of the prelude, it rushed up to the heights like a flash of lightning. Now it was the turn of the apprentices to wait, and that for twenty-six bars. To occupy themselves they took their brooms and swept the floor of the stage. Never before or afterwards in the history of the Bayreuth Festival Theatre was it cleaned so thoroughly.

My pleasure in the performance had gone. At the end of the act I dashed, white with rage, to Siegfried. I found him smiling and satisfied, making nothing of the incident.

I expected the international press to show indignation at this occurrence, which at Bayreuth seemed incredible. But there was not a single word of blame. This was because with the last note of the first act all the critics and reporters had immediately raced off to the town to the few telephones that were to be found, to be the first to describe the "sensation" of the re-opening of Bayreuth. Not one of them seemed to have heard the second act.

I was not wrong in believing that a performance of *Die Meistersinger* more in consonance with my wishes could easily be imagined; a stubborn curtain was not the only trouble.

The orchestra was excellent, the management of the chorus by Rüdel splendid, the scenery and production of Siegfried Wagner throughout skilful and superior. His talent, especially in managing crowds, was indisputable.

Still another force was emphatically effective in Bayreuth and should not be underestimated—an audience extremely knowledgeable in artistic matters, which did not let any refinement pass unnoticed or any blunder escape uncensured. There were many here who were a match for the chemist from Garmisch who, on a visit in Vienna to Richard Strauss, his neighbour and friend, pointed out a faulty third trumpet in the second act of *Die Meistersinger*—quite correctly, as the latter emphasised with approval. "Must I learn from a fellow who concocts poison," said Strauss to me, "that after half a century of study I still have not mastered the score!" I, too, after a rehearsal had to acknowledge, in reply to the criticism of a Hamburg solicitor, that my first violins did not emphasise clearly enough two quavers and a following triplet.

Besides many foreigners for whom Bayreuth meant nothing less than a place of pilgrimage, the audiences consisted of Germans from every part of the country and of every class. Intelligent, experienced and attentive sympathy on the part of the listeners is an essential need for an ideal artistic event. Here we had it.

Face to face with a unique success in the Festival Theatre, all criticism might well be silent. There were moments in which the spirit of Richard Wagner—that phenomenon which, as Thomas Mann says, "if considered as an artistic power was almost unequalled, perhaps the greatest talent in all the history of art"—could be felt lingering among us.

Where else could one see the meadow where the festival is held in the last act of *Die Meistersinger* so truly *festal*, as it spread out here before us, splendid and rich, faithful to Richard Wagner's instructions! Where were the slightest dynamic or scenic directions of the "master"—as he was called at Wahnfried in Byzantine fashion—followed and cared for as here!

When, in the second act of *Götterdämmerung*, Gunther's retainers "rush on hastily by different paths" as their creator says—when instead of a group of ponderous, bored choristers who must be careful not to get entangled in the wooden and pasteboard hills, a happy, unrestrained troop of wild young giants shout joyfully in glorious tones:

"Good luck and blessing smile on the Rhine, since Hagen, the grim Hagen, is so merry."[1]

Oh yes, then we were merry, too. Then we held our breath; we recognised genius.

With all the greater sorrow I always discovered how perfec-

[1] Gross Glück und Heil lacht nun dem Rhein
Da Hagen, der grimme, so lustig mag sein.
Götterdämmerung, Act II.

tion—so near, almost within our grasp—was thrown lightly away through obstinate persistence and a wrong idea of loyalty.

As in Dresden, what was lacking in Bayreuth, and only too often spoiled the whole impression, was individual singers. Nothing could be more incomprehensible, for at that time there was not a stage artist who would not have thrust himself forward to collaborate in the Festival.

Even then it was still not easy to find those who were really the best. One could not take whoever came, without consideration; one had to search and search again. Siegfried Wagner rightly recognised that not only the voice but the whole personality of the opera performer must be reckoned up. A Siegfried, for instance, must be tall and slim, and not weigh a hundred and forty kilos. An Evchen must be a young girl. Mine was not; though musically gifted she certainly was nearly as heavy as that. Of the many demands which are made on a singer, this one, which is quite justifiable, is only rarely fulfilled.

Toscanini, too, who had better luck with his engagement for *Tannhäuser* in 1930 than I had with *Die Meistersinger*, could not overlook the fact that his handsome performer of the title role sang as if the Festival Theatre belonged to a second-class town.

There were one or two ideal artists already on the spot. Others, in no way inferior, were waiting to be called upon. Why did this not happen?

What was vexatious and even tragic was that Wahnfried turned a deaf ear to all this. Loyalty was exaggerated at the expense of art. What they loved—how unlike the eternal revolutionary, whom Bayreuth had to thank for its existence —was to rely on a definite staff of singers and to approve of everything that "our" or "our splendid . . ." offered them. At my critical remarks and efforts at improvement obstinately repeated over and over again, they simply smiled.

Although we could not agree on this critical question, they liked me, at Wahnfried. One day I was taken to Frau Cosima. She was lying on a sofa and, in spite of her eighty-eight years, had an impressive head and magnificent eye. As so often happens with old people, she lived in a world of the past. Although I was presented to her as the conductor of *Die Meistersinger*, her first question was what I thought of Hans Richter's conducting? She further wanted to know my opinion of Marianne Brandt, Scaria and other great artists who had departed this life years before. I extricated myself from the situation as best I might.

At a later performance of *Die Meistersinger*, Frau Cosima, at her earnest wish, was taken to the only box in the Festival Theatre; it was at the disposal of the family. She listened attentively to one act.

After the first performance I was heartily invited to conduct the same work at Bayreuth in 1925.

I had hardly returned to Dresden when I began worrying away again in an attempt to get better singers placed at my disposal. I left no stone unturned. Again I had not the slightest success.

In the winter, Siegfried Wagner came to Dresden to conduct in the Gewerbehaus. Among other things he played a symphonic poem of his own composition which was called *Happiness*. He felt obliged to explain its contents beforehand to the audience in a spoken address. If his conception—opinions differed on this—was lacking in originality, his conclusion was not; true happiness is a hero's death!

Here, again, I was of a different opinion. Ten years had not gone by since I had seen hundreds of young men falling by my side at Ypres. Not one of them considered this death as the greatest happiness of his life.

After Siegfried had set forth this ideal I understood why, a few months before, he had invited me to Wahnfried with the remark that I should meet there "the greatest German". He meant General Ludendorff, and was honestly surprised that I showed no interest in meeting him and thought a rehearsal of *Die Meistersinger* more important.

Now I suddenly remembered the swastika which I had seen

for the first time in my life on the walls and fences in the neighbourhood of Wahnfried. The sight did not then leave more than a certain uncomfortable feeling.

Siegfried went away without his visit having led to any clarification of the situation. Everything was to remain as it was. To him, my indispensable wish to improve the *ensemble* of the singers appeared only the whim of a congenial but overzealous fellow.

In the specially exacting Dresden season of 1925 I had no further interval to give to clear consideration and important decisions. But the nearer the summer came the more my uneasiness increased as well as the wish not to return to Bayreuth until a thorough alteration could be effected there. If this did not take place my work would be without meaning and would rob me of happiness and enthusiasm, sources of strength which I, perhaps more than many of my colleagues, needed for my work to be profitable. Much too late I gave up all hope of a change of spirit in Wahnfried, and a few weeks before the beginning of rehearsals at Bayreuth wrote to Siegfried to cry off.

With this step I severely wounded him, which I regret to this day, the more so that he only survived my fleeting appearance in Bayreuth a few years. Siegfried was a kind, friendly creature who could never hurt anyone and whom I wish I had not hurt.

Muck took over the *Meistersinger* in the 1925 Festival in my place, and Rüdel used a lot of bad language.

My views remained unaltered.

Since then a second war has broken out over the world which has laid Germany for the most part in ruins. The modest red house on the Festival Hill was spared. Will the spirit of Richard Wagner once more take up its abode there?[1]

[1] The Bayreuth Festivals were resumed in 1950.

Chapter Ten

THE YEARS IN DRESDEN
1925-1933

Attend in particular to the two following
truths: first that outward things do not touch
our souls, but remain immovably external to
them. The peace of your soul is only disturbed
if you yourself permit it. And secondly: that
everything you see changes rapidly and
eventually will no longer exist. . . .
Always bear in mind: the universe is
transformation, life is illusion.

MARCUS AURELIUS

WHEN in 1924 the political disturbances in Germany had
been brought to a satisfactory end by the establishment
of the *rentenmark* and other economic reforms, things became
noticeably quieter, an advantage to music which had been
seriously involved in these troubles.

In the Chancellor, Gustav Stresemann, the country found for
a few years a great statesman whose self-sacrificing courage and
spirituality seemed to promise an honourable future to the
nation which was so torn by faction. The fact that he died
prematurely was one of the many events fraught with tragedy
of which German history is so full. A period of tranquillity,
due to Stresemann's wise policy, seemed to promise an enduring
cultural future; no one suspected that these were to be the last
years before it was destroyed.

It was thanks to Reucker, the Generalintendant, that immediately after he had taken up his post, the connection of Richard
Strauss with the Dresden State Opera, which had been interrupted for many years, was resumed. Almost all his operas had
been first performed at Dresden, under Ernst von Schuch;
their success and that of the great conductor had been brilliant.

169

Strauss now entrusted us with the world *première* of his chamber opera, *Intermezzo*.

The clever and experienced composer knew very well what advantages Dresden afforded for the introduction of his works to the stage. To the world-wide fame of its splendid orchestra Dresden could add such attractions as a restless capital like Berlin, with its excessive profusion of artistic events and ephemeral sensations, could not offer. In Dresden there was a kind of aristocratic unity and calm which was a great help to the works which were to be presented. All the light was focused on one point, resulting in an extraordinary brilliance.

Strauss knew that this unusual spirit of concentration was shared by the overworked press critics. In the charming idyllic atmosphere of Old Dresden, which had now returned for a few deceptive happy years, these harassed and disintegrated people were for once not in a distracted mood. They did not have to rush breathlessly to the performance from great distances at the last moment, but stayed comfortably in the well-known Hotel Bellevue near the Opera House. There they could study the work under consideration in complete tranquillity, could exchange opinions with their professional colleagues from all over the world, or if an eccentric among them was seized with the desire, he could enjoy the charms of Saxon Switzerland or the Erzgebirge as if he had come for a holiday and not on business.

This holiday mood took possession of the critics as well as the public, like a slight, pleasant intoxication. Who that has ever taken part in a Dresden *première* could deny it? In the unimaginable misery that reigns to-day in Germany and elsewhere there must be sad memories of those cheerful and easy-going days, especially among those Englishmen and Americans who year after year used to like to come to Dresden.

Richard Strauss knew how to make the best use of these advantages. His artistic needs for *Intermezzo* were met by the engagement of Lotte Lehmann, whom he valued highly, for the chief woman's part—that of Frau Hofkapellmeister Storch, alias Strauss; and by the promise given to the poet-composer to represent on the stage as realistically as possible his luxurious Garmisch home, where the greater part of the action takes place. On account of the intimate character of the work the performances on this occasion were transferred to the Schauspielhaus.

I much enjoyed studying the score, as the musical construction of the work shows a careful workmanship and a masterly power which must necessarily captivate a musician. I was much less pleased by the exhibitionism of the libretto written by Richard Strauss himself and based on his own experiences, even though Max Reinhardt once described it to me as "highly talented". When at the end of the opera the married pair—the Strausses—sing a sentimental cantilena in F sharp major after repeated domestic quarrels, "All the same it's a happy marriage", I felt embarrassed. Still, it was amusing to study the flowing, airy music, put together with such a sure hand, and to perform it with a masterly orchestra and first-class solo singers.

It was now a great pleasure to enter into closer personal relations with Richard Strauss, whom I had so far only come across casually. He arrived in Dresden at the end of October 1924 for the last rehearsals, and it soon became apparent that musically we understood each other admirably. Strauss spoke very frankly on professional and artistic questions. Not only did he willingly accept my critical objections, but he often asked me for my candid opinion of various details of the composition.

Among the important musicians with whom I have had closer personal acquaintance, Richard Strauss takes a peculiar place. Even his appearance and bearing, simple as they seemed, were ambiguous. If one recalls to memory his head, which so often fascinated the caricaturists, with its bullet forehead and almost expressionless watery blue eyes, on the top of a tall, lanky, slightly stooping body, he appears sometimes, and especially in his youthful portraits, to be simple, almost insignificant. But he could adopt a majestic bearing and, instead of looking commonplace and unimportant, display the superior simplicity of genius. In the same way his conducting shows a strange mixture, peculiar to him, of apathy and masterly directness which is not without an element of suggestion. This style of conducting practically never appears exciting but it *can* arouse excitement in the hearer. Then there seems to be direct contact with genius.

But the real secret of his success is not betrayed either by the precise movements of his baton, the balanced economy of his gestures or the calm expression on the face of this tall, well-groomed man.

Strauss was already in his sixties when I came into this closer contact with him, and my impressions are only of his later years. In his youth he is said to have conducted with unusual vivacity and temperament and often with actual violence.

In spite of his healthy complexion, the result of his regular life and his unforced joviality, Strauss was not in the least unsophisticated. At the first glance he appeared a *grand seigneur*: he might have been taken for the president of a bank. No one would have imagined he was an artist, and the most sparkling and many-sided talent in the whole range of modern music. Anyone looking at Reger would at once have taken him for a choir-master who should have been sitting at an organ.

No one, however, admired Strauss's genius, his technical mastery of orchestration, more than Reger, who was a hundredfold more profound a musician, though a greater contrast cannot be imagined between the mystical Reger full of profound religious feeling, and the earth-bound, worldly Strauss. Strauss reciprocated the other's high esteem and recognised unreservedly the ease and contrapuntal mastery of Reger's creative work. Strauss wrote to Reger, as Richard Wagner had once written to Liszt, that he envied him his tremendous abilities. Both Bavarians were, moreover, at one in their low opinion of Gustav Mahler as a composer, in which I did not agree with them. It so chanced that they both expressed their opinion to me, in almost the same words and in the same Bavarian dialect: "Well, Busch, as for Mahler he's not really a composer at all—he's simply a very great conductor."[1]

[1] "Sö, Busch, der Mahler, dös is überhaupt gar ka Komponist. Dös is bloss a ganz grosser Dirigent."

The lack of genuinely warm feeling which Strauss's music often shows was recognised by the composer himself; he knew exactly the places where his music became sentimental and trashy. Nothing annoyed him more than when conductors, among them some quite famous ones, wallowed in his lyrical outpourings and thus unpleasantly brought his sins before his eyes. He himself, the older he grew, passed ever more indifferently and unemphatically over such passages when conducting, as if he were ashamed of having composed them. His inconsistency showed itself in his continuing to write such things.

In Garmisch he played me his *Aegyptische Helena* which was to have its world *première* at Dresden, and asked for my sincere opinion. I did not hesitate to say, amongst other things, that I thought Daud's song in D flat major was cheap and that he ought to weigh such "inspirations" more carefully. He in no way disputed this criticism but actually repeated it with enjoyment to his wife, who had just come into the room, but then added with disdainful cynicism: "That's what's wanted for the servant girls. Believe me, dear Busch, the general public would not go to *Tannhäuser* if it didn't contain 'Oh, Star of Eve' or to the *Walküre* without 'Winter Storms'. Well, well, that's what they want."

The puzzle of Strauss, who in spite of his marvellous talents is not really penetrated and possessed by them like other great artists but, in fact, simply wears them like a suit of clothes which can be taken off at will—this puzzle neither I nor anyone else has yet succeeded in solving. His decided inclination towards material things made him an outspoken defender of capitalism, and with his complete disinclination to any sacrifice, the sworn enemy of social changes. His materialistic pleasures, even including his philistine enjoyment of his famous game of skat at which he was very seldom beaten, often seemed to be nearer his heart than his music.

But it became apparent that this impression was misleading when one met him quietly and intimately; for instance, in conversation about his favourite composer, Mozart. I remember once going through Mozart's clarinet concerto in my room at the Opera House with the first clarinet of the Dresden orchestra, when Richard Strauss came in. He was there for the *première* of one of his operas. We talked for a long time after this rehearsal about the marvellous Mozart. Strauss declared that his G minor string quintet was the summit of all music.

He himself had been an excellent pianist and was fond of telling how he had played one of Mozart's piano concertos under Hans von Bülow at Meiningen. He was always urging me to arrange for a series of performances of all Mozart's twenty-eight piano concertos, each one, he said, more beautiful than the last. "The best thing would be," he added, "for you to leave the conducting alone. Play them all yourself and improvise the cadenzas."

Since 1924 Richard Strauss had become a regular visitor at Dresden. Besides the world *premières* of *Intermezzo* and *Die Aegyptische Helena*, all his other operas were in the repertory, for the most part in newly studied performances which he himself conducted as a guest. The only exception was his first opera, *Guntram*, the score of which was buried by the composer himself in the garden of the house at Garmisch and lies under a tombstone with the inscription: "Here lies Guntram, a worthy and virtuous youth cruelly slain by his own father's symphonic orchestra."

His predilection for stopping in Dresden was increased by an invitation to the artist, tired of hotel life, from a middle-aged art-loving bachelor, a friend of ours, to stay at his beautiful, cultured home. In these surroundings, which suited his domestic habits and where he was looked after by an excellent servant instead of indifferent waiters, Richard Strauss could enjoy all the comforts which were afforded by the household of Albert Sommer, our then very wealthy Jewish friend, and felt particularly happy.

In the music room of this house, in February 1933, he read us the libretto of his *Schweigsame Frau*. Then he sat down at the piano, took his note-book out of his pocket, and played us the end of the work.

The relations between Strauss and myself had become very cordial, indeed friendly, and were to become even closer from his having dedicated his *Arabella* jointly to Dr. Reucker and me as representing the Dresden Opera. Strauss acknowledged my co-operation as conductor of his works on every opportunity with extraordinary, almost extravagant warmth. On my side, I admired his artistic power and his amazing talents too much to be seriously put off by his less attractive characteristics. They were exhibited with such ingenuous openness, were so free from cunning or bad-tempered calculation, that one could really hardly take them in bad part.

Events which had taken place before the *première* of *Die Aegyptische Helena* should have been a warning to me; they showed how unscrupulous Strauss was capable of being. But I did not realise how far this was sure to lead when the time came. He who in his inmost heart was in direct opposition to National-Socialist ideology had long before anticipated in practice one of its dogmas: "Right is what is of use to me."

In the year 1927, on an invitation from Walter Damrosch, I conducted for the first time the New York Symphony Orchestra, founded and led by this veteran of American conductors. It later amalgamated with the Philharmonic Orchestra. This invitation was repeated for the 1927–28 season, when I was at the head of the orchestra for three months.

My most noteworthy experience during this visit was my meeting with Yehudi Menuhin. On my journey to New York I had already read in the papers of the great success of this boy, at that time nine years old. It was proposed that he should be the soloist at one of my concerts and, in fact, the child wanted to play Beethoven's concerto. I thought I could not consent to this choice. "Jackie Coogan is not allowed to act the part of Hamlet," I said.

I advised a Mozart concerto. But finally Menuhin's father persuaded me to hear the Beethoven concerto, accompanied on the piano. Yehudi had never before played it in public with an orchestra; I could always refuse when I had heard it.

175

In my room on the thirty-third floor of the Gotham Hotel the fair, charming boy appeared with his teacher, Louis Persinger, and his father, who never left his side. He took out his fiddle and played so gloriously and with such complete mastery that by the second *tutti* I was already won over. This was perfection.

The first rehearsal with the orchestra aroused such enthusiasm among the musicians that, though it was not customary at that time, I placed the concerto at the end of the programme. No orchestra and no conductor could be in a position to compete with the overpowering effect of this first appearance. Not a creature in the Carnegie Hall would have had ears for any music whatever, after Yehudi had played the last bar of the Rondo.

That feeling of anticipation of which I have spoken in another connection now seized the gigantic City of New York, although beyond the inner circle nothing was known of Yehudi. The house was sold out and everyone was in the excited state of tension that precedes an experience confidently expected to be really great.

On the day before the concert I was invited to tea with the German-American banker, Goldman, and told him of the rehearsals with Menuhin, which were completely engrossing me. The charming old gentleman, who was unfortunately blind, had a deep understanding of music. He had not subscribed to all my concerts, some of which were rather indifferent, but now immediately ordered seats for the boy's first appearance. I saw how disappointed he was when he found there was not a single place to be had, so I placed my own box at the disposal of him and Mrs. Goldman.

The unparalleled success of Yehudi with the Beethoven concerto on that first night no one who was present will forget. Mr. Goldman resolved to give the child something to make him specially happy. This was the Stradivarius violin which Yehudi has played since that time.

In 1929 the Menuhin family came to Europe. On the advice of some American musicians, Yehudi's father wished his son

Adolf and Fritz Busch

Richard Strauss and Fritz Busch, 1925

to study for some time longer with my brother Adolf, who at that period was living at Bâle.

Yehudi now played in Dresden, under me, the three violin concertos—Bach's in E major, Beethoven's and Brahms'. Apart from the physical performance of this eleven-year-old boy, the technical, intellectual and musical perfection of his playing cannot be imagined. The experienced Saxon chamber music players, always inclined to belittle the performances of others and very seldom impressed, were so moved by this child's execution that many of them had tears in their eyes.

When the general rehearsal was over, Yehudi, whose father did not leave him unwatched for a moment, played after dinner with the same enthusiasm with our son Hans, who was a few years older than he was, and an electric railway.

After the triumphal concert we met the Menuhins, Mrs. Goldman and her friend, the celebrated lieder singer Elena Gerhart, at supper at the Hotel Bellevue. By Yehudi's special wish his new friend Hans had to sit beside him. Hans was delighted to be able to put his few words of broken English to use.

At table in the course of the evening I spoke a few sentences with a full heart, still under the influence of the concert, of the responsibility which fate had placed in the hands of this wonderful child's parents and teacher. I spoke in German, which everyone except Yehudi knew, with the express intention that the boy should not understand what was said about him. He, who up to now only knew the German words, "It is decreed by God Himself",[1] immediately noticed my solemn gravity, to which he was quite unaccustomed with me. When I had finished he smiled shyly at me and said to Mrs. Goldman: "I knew that Mr. Busch was a very good conductor but when I heard him speak I thought that he could also be a wonderful Rabbi!"

I effected the connection with Adolf with great difficulty, as he had scruples about teaching infant prodigies. He had had unpleasant experiences, not with the prodigies or the in-

[1] "Es ist bestimmt in Gottes Rat." First words of a song by Mendelssohn.

fants, but with the parents. As a rule it was their love of money-making that seemed to justify his scepticism.

As I could not get away, my wife went to Berlin and took the young violinist to the older one, who said to her before Yehudi's entrance: "If he wishes to become a good musician we can talk matters over; but if they just want to make money let him keep out."

Then this first acquaintance at the Hotel Adlon took the same turn as with me at the performance of the Beethoven concerto in New York, and Adolf undertook to teach the boy.

It was agreed that Yehudi, after beginning his studies with Adolf, should at first appear on only a few occasions each year. One of these exceptional occasions was to be a concert in Berlin.

In a letter, I approached Frau Louise Wolff, whom I had known for years as the energetic and forcible manager of the widespread Herman Wolff concert agency and whom I specially valued for her vitality and her sharp, witty tongue. "Königin Louise" occupied a dominating position in the German world of concerts at that time.

With a heavy heart she had departed from her fundamental rule and decided on her side to undertake the unusually high fee and other expenses of an introductory concert with the Philharmonic Orchestra. I shared the responsibility for the arrangement, for Louise Wolff had made her participation dependent on my judgment. She expected that the announcement of the boy whose name was already internationally celebrated, would suffice to fill the hall. But the spoilt people of Berlin held off and waited. Without much ado the clever woman, saying nothing to me, published the enthusiastic letter I had written her about Yehudi, as a feuilleton in the *Berliner Tageblatt*, and thus was quickly successful in selling all the Philharmonic tickets.

I was joyfully awaiting the day on which I should present Yehudi in Berlin. Just as I was starting for the rehearsal I received the news that my father had suddenly died of a heart attack. I immediately cancelled my engagement and Bruno Walter undertook to conduct in my place.

My father's death was in keeping with his restless life. Once again he had wished to move. A newly-built house in Bochum contained a fine workshop in which he wished to make his fiddles. Early one morning he ran quickly up the steep street to install his instruments and tools. When he reached the house he said to the builders: "Boys, I don't feel well. I shall lie down. Just push a violin case under my head so that I can sleep for a bit." And so, on the floor of his workshop he fell asleep for ever.

My father's peculiar attitude towards life was to be once more apparent in his death. As I was travelling towards Bochum to pay my last respects to my good father, as the eldest son, I seemed to see before my eyes his life and personality. And so I found myself somewhat embarrassed as to how to carry out my father's often expressed last wishes. More than once, in fact, he had said to me: "Take care that when I am dead the hearse goes at a gallop. All my life I have had to run after other people; for once let them run after me."

If this wish, like so many others of his, remained unfulfilled, all the same his funeral brought him quite a success.

When we were children we often begged our father, who could not bear the clergy of any creed, to show us how an old minister preached in a simple-minded fashion on the text: "Two of the disciples were going to Emmaus."

"Dear brethren," thus solemnly began our father, standing on the table wrapped in a black cloth, "were there really *two*? Could there not have been three or even four? No, there were two. It is expressly written. *Two* disciples . . ." and a lot more similar nonsense which we children thought immensely funny.

When in sincere sorrow we were all standing round the grave for the last farewell to our father, an old toothless minister made his appearance, opened the Bible and began to declaim in pathetic accents: "Two disciples were going to Emmaus." We thought we saw father standing before us and nodding to us with a smile: "Don't take it all so seriously!"

I saw Yehudi again in Bâle when he had begun his studies with Adolf. Two equally gifted sisters, also with Biblical names, Hephzibah and Yalta, played the piano and were having lessons with Rudolf Serkin.

At the end of 1929 I went to London to conduct Yehudi's concert there. Mr. Menuhin had considerable difficulty in getting permission from the English authorities for his son to perform, as by English law the professional appearance of young people is prohibited after a certain hour at night. In the end the concert did take place on a Sunday evening at the Queen's Hall and had as brilliant a success as the earlier concerts in New York, Dresden and Berlin.

What I wished for Yehudi with all my heart was the complete tranquillity in which, in fortunate cases, an infant prodigy can develop into a master. This boon was bestowed in former times on Joseph Joachim. In his youth his father and discerning counsellors had assured him the leisure to mature quietly in the dangerous years while development was taking place. Intercourse with great personalities such as Ferdinand David, Mendelssohn, Robert and Clara Schumann and, later, Liszt, Wagner and Brahms, gave a comprehensive musical knowledge to a mind already prepared to receive it. Thus it was that Joachim became the most commanding violinist of his century.

In spite of all warnings to the contrary, Yehudi began prematurely to develop into a virtuoso. He began a nomadic life that disinterested friends would have wished to spare the child.

On the day after the London concert, a Monday, I missed the train to the Continent owing to the heavy traffic in Piccadilly. But I wanted at all costs to be in Dresden on Tuesday. In spite of the stormy autumn weather I therefore took a place in the next plane, which called forth violent opposition from a woman friend from Stuttgart who had just come to the concert from Liverpool. Like Tolstoi, I cannot bear a woman's tears. At her weeping and wailing I crossly gave back the ticket I had already bought. A few hours later I read in the evening paper in large headlines that the plane in question had run into a hill in the fog immediately on leaving Croydon, and the crew and all the passengers had been burnt to death.

My second visit to America had led to contact and friendship with many intelligent Americans, chiefly of course musicians. These personal connections combined with the fame of the Dresden State Opera led Damrosch—still full of youthful enterprise and new ideas—to a very interesting scheme. He stirred up the Juilliard Foundation with its great wealth, to decide to form an Opera School in Dresden for members of the American Opera. A selection of several young American singers with talent were to go there to become acquainted with German traditions of opera and, by taking part in the performances, acquire experience and a knowledge of style. There would also be opportunities for native talent.

This generous idea which I enthusiastically thought I would bring to Dresden as an agreeable present from the States, was frustrated by the narrowmindedness and greedy local patriotism of the Saxons. The uncomprehending amazement with which I heard the selfish and petty arguments which they brought against the plan showed my lack of acquaintance with human shabbiness, nearly forty as I was.

Instead of this undertaking which had miscarried, a private course of study for singers was organised by the Americans based on reciprocal esteem. This was an advantage both for Dresden and for us. From the summer of 1928 onwards the New York teacher of singing, William Vilonat, accompanied by his clever assistant Sidney Dietch, came to Dresden every year. Many of his countrymen regularly did the same.

Always in search of talent, and in particular interested in good voices, I had entered into relations with well-known teachers of singing in New York who, on their side, had everything to gain by bringing their finished pupils to me.

Tragi-comic experiences with many who undertook to train voices had convinced me that this profession was made up of a peculiar species of human being. In Leipzig a savage made his pupils push a heavy Steinway grand piano from one room to another before beginning a lesson in order to "stimulate their breath action". This was nothing compared to the æsthete and fanatic of Stuttgart of whom it was maintained that his method necessitated the use of a spittoon! His pupils had to employ this utensil before they opened their mouths to sing—for instance—Mozart's "Within these sacred bowers".[1] And the great Lilli Lehmann herself was so fanatically convinced of the excellence of her principles of teaching that she forced a pronounced deep contralto who, by my advice, took lessons from her, to sing both arias of the Queen of the Night to obtain full mastery of her vocal powers. When the unhappy girl, after a year of work, sang me "Vengeance storms within my bosom"[2] in a thin, trembling voice, I could only agree that she was quite right.

If this mistake of a great artist demanding from others her own extraordinary powers of execution was to some extent excusable, much that could never be forgiven and was actually criminal took place in the sphere of singing lessons. The charlatan was hard to distinguish from the idealist—the ignoramus from the master who was never tired of searching for the laws governing that complicated instrument, the human voice.

Vilonat was among the masters. Conscious knowledge was united in him to intuitive certainty, enabling him to recognise the possibilities and limits of a voice and to bring out all its quality to the last ounce. His many-sided culture, his charming sense of humour combined with open-heartedness and his unusual gift of fascination made him extremely attractive.

A troop of worshipping girls and youths used to follow him to Dresden, bringing with them an atmosphere like the one in Hermann Bahr's *Konzert*. It was only the serious dignity of this unusual, energetic man that kept the young people within the bounds of propriety.

Every year, at the end of the Dresden course, the pupils sang in front of an audience at the Opera House. A young, good-

[1] In diesen heil'gen Hallen. *Die Zauberflöte*.
[2] Rache tobt in meinem Herzen. *Die Zauberflöte*.

looking man began at once the first bar of Wolfram's "Like death's foreboding twilight shrouds the meadows"[1] without the usual stage fright, in such a fine voice, and with such beautiful expression that I at once offered him an engagement. It was Nelson Eddy who, to our regret, did not accept the contract— a case that did not happen every day at Dresden. It seems that Eddy, so I heard, later made a lot of money in Hollywood!

In June 1925 the Dresden Opera again took part in the Zürich Festival, this time with Strauss's *Intermezzo*. Afterwards, Arturo Toscanini was expected to bring a concert tour with the Scala Orchestra to its conclusion there.

One summer evening an enormous crowd of people blocked up the traffic in front of the concert room, which was not open. We learnt that Toscanini, in consequence of an unfortunate contretemps, had cancelled the concert. My Zürich colleague, Volkmar Andreae, knew that he had gone with friends and musicians to a small Italian tavern, and we followed him there.

In a few minutes Toscanini and I were absorbed in the most animated conversation on musical questions, although to this day I cannot understand how. We both suffered from the results of the Tower of Babel. Our exchange of ideas was the product of Toscanini's Wagner German and my smattering of broken Italian, helped out on both sides by loud singing and violent gesticulation. The contact we made here lasted for twenty years, with an improved linguistic foundation. I may say it was friendship, until Toscanini, with increasing age, silently withdrew, except for a specially intimate circle, from those who did not force themselves upon him.

I met Toscanini repeatedly, not only at the Scala, where I gave a set of concerts supported by my brother and Serkin as solo players, but also in other Italian guest performances, for instance in Rome, Florence and Venice as well as Dresden and many other places. Once the Maestro appeared in his car unannounced and in great secrecy for a performance of *Don Giovanni* in Dresden, a new production of which had caused

[1] "Wie Todesahnung Dämmrung deckt die Lande" *Tannhäuser.*

183

some sensation. As in spite of that I could not stop finding fault with the way the opera was performed, in general and in particular, Toscanini replied, with a comforting, pious ejaculation: "Caro amico, io lo faccio da quaranta-tre anni!"

Again he appeared at Dresden unexpectedly, to be present at a performance of *La Forza del Destino* by Verdi. It was at that time quite forgotten in Germany and was given a new performance by me in Franz Werfel's somewhat free but beautifully poetical translation of the text. Toscanini came expressly for this performance because in Dresden it had an unusual success, while when directed by him in Italy it had always been, he said, a complete fiasco. Every Italian thought it had the evil eye and crossed his fingers to avert it.

While I was standing talking to Toscanini, Georgi, the theatre attendant, came up and said: "We can't have the Force of Destiny to-day, sir, because Fräulein Seinemeyer's ill. We must give *Die Aegyptische Helena*."[1]

The evil eye! No use crossing one's fingers!

Apart from this one piece of bad luck *La Forza del Destino* was one of those productions of opera in which one feels near the ideal of the art. We had in the unforgettable Meta Seinemeyer, who unfortunately died young, a wonderful interpreter of Leonora and, indeed, of other parts of Verdi and less important Italian composers of a lyrical, emotional character. In Giordano's *André Chénier* she was a touching Madeleine. If in proficiency she was not equal to Rethberg, of whom her voice reminded me, she had instead an incomparable spiritual quality which people like to call "tears in the voice". Nothing better could be written on her tombstone than the last words of *La Forza del Destino*: "The soul lives."[2]

On his lucky evenings the Dresden Opera also possessed the best partner for this singer—an Alvaro, Don Carlos, Othello or André Chénier—one whose unique combination of appear-

---

[1] "Herr Generalmusigdirecder, heide is keene *Machd des Schigsals*, weil die Frollein Seinemeyer krank is. Mr soll 'n de ägybdische Helena gäh 'm."
[2] Die Seele lebt. German version of *La Forza del Destino*.

ance and voice would have led him to develop into an ideal performer if his unfortunate character and fatal weakness had not brought the career of this most lovely tenor and handsomest of men on the German opera stage to a bad end.

His bodily gifts and talent seemed to make it worth while to undertake the thankless and in the end tragically useless task of using him for our opera. In the battle with all the evil powers which fought over him I succeeded in wresting from him a series of performances which could hardly be equalled, even though they were poor compared with his possibilities and were always doubtful, always unreliable and often hung in the balance on the stage itself.

The company increased in numbers and improved considerably in the course of time. Among distinguished performers of individual parts who had been drawn in by Schuch and were now at the height of their powers were the coloratura soprano Erna Berger, the mezzo-soprano Martha Fuchs, the tenor Max Lorenz, as well as the powerful bass Ivar Andresen, who came to an untimely end.

Supported by clever producers as, for instance, the experienced Dr. Otto Ehrhardt, and by Reucker's own expert guidance, we were able to produce a repertory which in some years included seventy-five different operas and ballets. Scene painters such as Fanto and Mahnke provided a worthy background. There was a season in which we brought out ten different masterpieces of Verdi. From Handel's *Xerxes* to Stravinsky's *Petrouchka*, one could hear practically everything of value within the sphere of opera, including ballet.

In fact, the Dresden opera reached such a splendour and musical perfection as a first-class German opera house was capable of within the framework of the existing system. If one remembers the long, breathless excitement produced by such works as *Boris*, *La Forza del Destino* or the gloomy grandeur of *Don Carlos*, the high spirits of *Falstaff*, *Don Giovanni* or a beautiful performance of *Cosi fan Tutte* assisted as a guest by the fine, musical Editha Fleischer-Engel, Toscanini's favourite singer, it was hard to find anything lacking. Only recently I met a competent American musician in a circle of colleagues and pupils to whom he was describing the Dresden Opera as something unimaginably beautiful, almost legendary.

It was, however, a reality. Looking back, I ask myself why there were so few moments when I felt completely happy. I might have been so more often if I had been only the first Kapellmeister, and not also the director who bore the responsibility for every detail.

In great world *premières* and individual new productions I could manage to keep approximately balanced the trembling scales of the manifold problems of opera. In the programme of everyday this was impossible. At that time I once said in a discussion of the opera that the warmest wish of an opera conductor was to give performances not daily but three times, or at most four times, a week, and spend the rest of his time in rehearsing. This was leading to what I later learnt by my experience abroad, in particular at the Colon Theatre in Buenos Aires, namely, that seasonal work has artistic advantages over the clumsy organisation of a German theatre.

During my long years of experience I became convinced that there is a widespread error in people's ideas about *Opera*. They are inclined to think it is an easily prepared food for the mind of the public—a notion which it is hardly possible to destroy. The opposite is the fact. The composite work we call *Opera* is in reality the most presumptuous and tricky product that the artistic propensity of man has ever brought forth. In a critical study of opera in 1932 a *connoisseur* remarked that there was no final solution to the problems which surround it. I agree with his conclusion: "Born from a paradox, opera will survive as a beautiful riddle."

Reucker and I, in a pamphlet we published after ten years' collaboration, said almost the same thing more prosaically: "Even in the most propitious circumstances the results of opera management will always suffer from the vast distance between what is attempted and what is attained."

186

Now, the circumstances in which I directed opera were never "propitious". I began this work at the moment a revolution was breaking out after a war that had been lost, and the ten years in Dresden must be called a period which "beginning in inflation ended in one of the greatest economic crises of all time".

Germany and all other countries had suffered a new blow of destiny in the Wall Street economic crisis. The depression in the world market forced the state to use the greatest thrift, the effects of which could be felt in Dresden more obviously than in the capital, Berlin. There they were inclined light-heartedly to overpay excellent singers who relied on their powers of attraction and often made unlimited demands. Reucker referred bitterly to "utmost limits" and "the necessity of retrenchment".

Another point concerned what had also been mentioned in our pamphlet—"the wearisome work in the service of the so-called 'performances in the repertory'." A comparison with Berlin and Vienna showed that besides the chief conductor, one or more kapellmeisters of the first rank were engaged. Not so in Dresden. If I rose to the heights in a successful performance of which I might well be proud, in the every-day routine of a performance of *Martha*, *Butterfly* or *Fra Diavolo* one often saw and heard opera as it should *not* be. The thought was repugnant to me that some cultivated member of the audience who yesterday had experienced the fulfilment of all his wishes in the Dresden Opera might, after sleeping off his happy intoxication, go to one of *those* performances which, after all, "are the real standard by which the level of a theatre with a varying programme can be measured."

This was not repugnant to my two colleagues at the conductor's desk. Cleverer than I, they reckoned with the existing circumstances. They were efficient men of routine, genuine successors of Reissiger, whom Richard Wagner describes so amusingly. In this direction it was useless to hope for improvement.

But economy was not the only brake to hold back development, for one could always hope to get free of it as once before.

187

A much greater hindrance was the entire system, shackled by tradition and custom, which was a barrier to the very necessary reforms.

In other state operas conditions were about the same, except for the difference I have mentioned that there several first kapellmeisters were at work. There would have been no sense in going to a different position, as I was asked to, first by Berlin, then repeatedly by Vienna.

In a German state theatre the artistic construction of the scenery, for instance, was made incredibly more difficult by the fact that it was entrusted to able and upright artisans. Having worked for the state all their lives they could not be dismissed so long as they did not steal the silver spoons. They certainly did their best, but neither imagination nor originality could be required of them, especially where some alien subject-matter was concerned. It cost me much trouble, strength and annoyance, though Reucker supported me through thick and thin, to bring in from outside progressive, superior painters and architects. As the result of these efforts we had Slevogt's designs for Mozart's *Don Giovanni*, beautiful but not in quite the same key—Kokoschka's scenery for Hindemith, Heckroth's *Don Carlos*, designs by Poelzig and Pretorius and the original, much disputed *Ring des Nibelungen* by Strnad, as well as the happy improvisations of the Russian Chudjakoff. But these were exceptions.

I made myself enemies, for I often could not hide my dissatisfaction and disapproval. Besides that, in my continued search for what was new and for opportune enlivening of the opera, I engaged the very gifted producer of the Schauspielhaus, Josef Gielen, and thus made bad blood in the State Opera.

With Reucker and Engel, I considered again and again how to achieve improvement. As above all the level of the everyday productions had to be improved, I sent up petition after petition that, with a corresponding reduction in my salary, a conductor like Leo Blech or Otto Klemperer should be engaged besides me, or at least a young kapellmeister with talents and enthusiasm. I would gladly have given up some of my leave to act as guest conductor if by so doing I could have succeeded in offering only such performances as corresponded with what Wagner demanded for a complete operatic work of art.

I tried to reach something like what Mahler in Vienna and Toscanini at the Scala in Milan had achieved—the complete reorganisation of the opera, without consideration for age-old personal interests, established powers or rights acquired by ancient custom.

My suggestions were in vain. The power of inertia was irresistible. The struggle to carry through my artistic wishes, if not always without success, ended in the course of years by wearing me down. Less and less often did the consciousness of "the vast distance between what is attempted and what is attained" fade from my mind.

Then I got to know Carl Ebert.

I saw his production of Mozart's *Entführung aus dem Serail* in the Berlin Opera of which he was the newly appointed producer, and the whole execution aroused my enthusiasm so much, in spite of occasional over-subtleties, that I now had only one idea—to work in association with that man.

Strangely enough, it happened that Ebert, who up to that time knew me as little as I knew him, had been inspired by the same wish, after watching me at the conductor's desk in Dresden. On the first opportunity he offered me the post of Musikdirektor at his opera house, but I could not at first decide to leave Dresden. Much had been started there with great enthusiasm and not yet brought to completion. In spite of disappointments and success alike I was governed by the feeling that I had still much to give to this, perhaps the most distinguished of German artistic centres.

On the occasion of the Salzburg Festival of 1932 I worked with Ebert for the first time. I was to conduct Mozart's *Entfuhrung aus dem Serail* there, and had made Ebert's engagement as producer a condition. We understood each other so perfectly that he on his side invited me to prepare and conduct as a guest a completely new production of Verdi's *Ballo in Maschera* in his theatre. The third in the alliance was the clever scene-painter Caspar Neher who, through his combination of innocence and craftiness, was to afford us many cheerful hours.

Already in Salzburg Ebert and I had begun a lively exchange of our ideas for the *Ballo*. For once, I was able to build up an opera production in the smallest detail and with free imagination and complete respect for the work, by the help of two men of the theatre of superior talent. These weeks of intensive preparation I reckon among the happiest experiences of my career. They also led to remarkable results in the coming years of my collaboration with the great producer.

Certainly differences of opinion between us were not lacking, when my impression was that Carl Ebert did violence to the music, whereas, to alter a pronouncement of Mozart's, "production should be the obedient daughter of music". But as we both understood how to subordinate personality to the matter in hand we always came to a good understanding again.

Carl Ebert, a big man of handsome appearance, not unconscious of this quality, had been a pupil of Max Reinhardt and a very good actor before he took up the post of Intendant, first in Darmstadt and then in Berlin. He went over to opera because he was specially fascinated by the connection between music and words. Just as I had been searching for a producer, he had been searching for a conductor.

The performance of *Un Ballo in Maschera* at the Berlin Opera was an event which people all over the world have remembered for long in unusual agreement, and which even to-day is not forgotten.

A very shrewd but somewhat surprising description of this evening was given by the critic of the *Frankfurter Zeitung*:

"The audience applauded as if in a frenzy. There was no trace of theatre weariness on this unusual night. There is still life in the drama if it is genuine, sappy, daemonic

drama. The daemon presided over Professor Ebert's opera
in Charlottenburg. They acted, mimed, played and sang
as if possessed. . . . Not an arm was stuck out in an operatic
pose. The masks were faces. After unveiling herself the
heart-broken Nemeth stands helpless, like no other despairing opera heroine. . . . A servant puts a light on the table
at the right moment and fills up the interval in the action
while the orchestra is playing. When the Signori are going
away servants run up and bring their cloaks, thus accelerating
the end of the act. After the assassination in the masked ball
all the masks, which have become unnecessary, are raised.
That is drama! . . . The guests in front stand petrified. But
quite at the back unearthly figures, shrouded in grey, go on
with the dance . . . until they too become aware that murder
has been done. Then at last all movement stops. And Richard
sings a swan song of pardon. A tragic scene! In Charlottenburg men of intellect are reduced to tears."

I think of this night as the first fulfilment for me in fourteen
years of working for opera, of unwavering cherished wishes.
Here the fact was verified that my pains and faith had not been
in vain, that opera has not been vanquished but can now, as
formerly, produce an effect, even a violent emotion.

In Dresden, this development was viewed with dissatisfaction. Nothing was easier to understand than the wish that this
success should have been obtained in their own house. For the
last time I hoped that the example thus set would have a good
effect in my aristocratic theatre, so rich in tradition.

In the autumn of 1932 in the Berlin theatre one full house
followed another. The interest in the *Ballo* was so lasting that
we might have had a long run—a proof of my theory, which
I was always bringing forward in Dresden, that productions of
outstanding quality pay best.

For intelligent circles in Berlin, no one of whom had missed
this performance, the evening meant the beginning of a new
operatic era. A vista had been opened out. But the Nazis
slammed the door shut.

Chapter Eleven

DISCUSSION WITH NATIONAL SOCIALISM
AND FAREWELL TO GERMANY

"Yesterday someone got into my plantation and
pulled everything up," said August.
"Pulled it up?"
"All the plants. There's not a single leaf left."
"Good gracious me! Did some animal get in?"
"Yes: a man."

(FROM "AUGUST WELTUMSEGLER"
BY KNUT HAMSUN)

IN the year 1930 I went for a few weeks to a sanatorium at
Nassau, in the neighbourhood of Coblenz. Everyday politics
had never particularly interested me, although the fate and
future of my country after the war always occupied my mind.
I had always kept away from party struggles. I thought with
Goethe "that it becomes a man better to do what is right than
to take trouble that what is right should be done."

One day I saw Nazi posters with swastikas and the notice
"No Jews admitted" announcing a meeting in the room of the
hotel in the little town. I went in and found the hall decorated
with red cloth and the usual emblems. Against the wall were
standing S.A. men, strong young fellows whose uniform I saw
for the first time. The only speaker—"Discussion not allowed"
—was a certain Reverend Münchmeyer who, even under the
forbearing Weimar Republic, had lost his position on account
of offences against morality but who, nonetheless, was thought
by the National Socialist Party good enough to represent the
constituency of Hesse-Darmstadt in the Reichstag. I remember
his dirty history, which was talked of there and got him called
by a witty social democrat member "the meat inspector".[1]

What Münchmeyer said was stupid, easily refuted chatter,

[1] Fleischbeschauer.

192

Fritz and Hans Peter Busch leave Germany, 1933

the lowest sort of appeal to the mob in style and expression. The peasants and men of the middle classes, at first hesitating, finally followed the speaker with increasing enthusiasm, and in the end he could claim a cheap success which I anticipated with painful anxiety. I went away in disgust.

It was the only meeting of the National Socialist Party I ever attended and I do not believe I missed anything by staying away from any others.

As a thorough German, on the other hand, I procured Hitler's *Mein Kampf* and read the book conscientiously. As will be seen later, this reading was useful to me. My instinctive aversion from the doctrines of the National Socialist Party became, after the study of this book, a conscious opposition. Although I knew that morals and politics were as a rule different things, in this case I could not remain silent. I felt it was not only my right but my duty to fight as unequivocally as possible against this completely amoral teaching.

What I said quite openly on the subject of National Socialism during the next two years was, as it appeared in March 1933, eagerly noted down by those around me, and finally resulted in an indictment that covered many pages of typewriting and was widely spread in the German theatre world before I succeeded with great difficulty in coming face to face with it. I could not deny that I had made the remarks which the informers of the Party had noted down with scrupulous exactness.

In the course of the year 1932 the Party realised that my cooperation in building up their third Reich could not be relied on. On the principle they had adopted—"He who is not for me is against me"—they gave up the attitude they had hitherto maintained of expectant benevolence and went over to the attack. The elections had given the Nazis an ever-increasing majority in the Saxon Landtag. Finally, this majority was big enough to be able to reject the budget of the state theatre, which had to be carried anew every year in sittings that lasted for several days, with the eager participation of Tom, Dick and Harry. My publicly-shown aversion led to an open attack in the National Socialist press, which was becoming ever more influential. The ways and means in which they proceeded against me as the responsible artistic head of the Dresden Opera is clearly described by Hitler in his book *Mein Kampf* on page 93 (13th Edition, 1932). In the following passage I only put *Nazi* instead of *Jewish* to show quite clearly in what form and on what lines such a battle may be conducted.

Hitler writes:[1]

"At first I was quite surprised when I realised how little time was necessary for this dangerous Great Power within the State (the Press) to produce a certain belief among the public even when in doing so the genuine will and convictions of the public were often completely misconstrued. It took the Press only a few days to transform some ridiculously trivial matter into an issue of national importance. . . . They succeeded in the magical art of producing names from nowhere within the course of a few weeks . . . at the same time old and tried figures . . . were so vilely abused that it looked as if their names would soon stand as permanent symbols of the worst kind of baseness or roguery. One had to study this infamous National Socialist" (Hitler says "Jewish") "method by which honourable people were besmirched with mud and filth in the form of low abuse and slander from hundreds and hundreds of quarters. . . . These highway robbers would grab at anything which might serve their ends. They would not rest until with their instinct for finding truffles they had sniffed out some petty item which could be used to destroy the reputation of their victim. But if the result of all this sniffing was that absolutely nothing derogatory was discovered in the private or public life of the victim they continued to hurl their slanders at him, not only in the firm belief that by repeating them something would stick in spite of a thousand denials, but also because the slanders could be re-echoed interminably, while the victim often found it impossible to fight against them."

To make myself understood I must give a few examples.

[1] Translation of *Mein Kampf* by James Murphy; Hurst & Blackett.

In 1932 I conducted a concert in Berlin with Miecislaw Horszowski, an excellent musician and pianist whom I had got to know in Milan, at Toscanini's. I took the Dresden State Orchestra with me. Although, owing to the excessive claims of the members of the orchestra, the scheme brought nothing but trouble and vexation I would not give it up. As the Dresden Opera performance took place at the same time the orchestra had to be supplemented. For this purpose Kutzschbach recruited the young men and girls who were pupils of the Saxon State Orchestra School. Whether as a joke or from absence of mind, when the girls asked him what they were to wear, he said, "Dinner jackets." This blunder was all the more harmless as, owing to the sunk orchestra pit, the "foolish virgins" could not be seen by the audience.

This—what does Hitler call it?—"ridiculously trivial matter", which took place in my absence and without my knowledge, nevertheless brought upon me a vote of no confidence from the Nazi Party in the Landtag. After the Nazi press had poured out their flood of "mud and filth in the form of low abuse and slander", Kutzschbach admitted his mistake, apologised to me and was prepared to make a public explanation. It did not seem to me to be worth the trouble.

I no longer wondered at finding headings in the Dresden scandalmongering press such as "The Man with the Peculiar Tendencies" and similar nonsense. Dresden held the record in the German gutter press for the number of papers of that sort.

It was the second prompter at the opera who was one of the sources of Nazi information which (see Hitler) "did not rest until with their instinct for finding truffles they had sniffed out some petty item which could be used to destroy the reputation of their victim". In the autumn of 1932 Reucker had engaged a certain Dr. Börner for this position. From the moment he entered the establishment indiscretions of every imaginable kind began to make their way into the open, dealing by no means only with me personally, but much more with the innermost and most confidential workings of the management as well as with the artistic side of the opera. Details known only to the initiated appeared the day after the proceedings in the local Nazi paper *Der Freiheitskampf*, with hateful comments.

In March 1933 the incognito of Herr Börner came to light in triumphant fashion. It appeared that he, though not a doctor, was in fact the highest Nazi informer—the "first cell"—who had been introduced into the state theatre.

Perhaps it was a mistake that I ignored those attacks in the press, whose untruthfulness would not have been difficult to prove. I considered them below my notice.

Invitations to join the NSDAP[1] came, as well as vulgar pin-pricks from the most different quarters. A few days before the decisive events, my wife refused to see an aristocratic party member, who then demanded in writing a "specified money contribution to the Cause". We answered brusquely that with the exception of the Salvation Army we supported no "Party", least of all his.

The National Socialist cells which they had formed in the Opera House and which exercised their activities among my closest collaborators, continued to provide rich material consistently used for abusive articles about me. I was soon tired of reading this stuff. I disliked Dresden more and more, and Carl Ebert's repeated summons began to weigh more with me.

I received yet another "summons" to Berlin. Somebody there, to my no small astonishment, shared my growing opinion that I should do better to leave Dresden. This person was Hermann Göring. Nine years before, in Stuttgart, we had made the acquaintance of the young twenty-three-year-old actress, Emmy Sonnemann, with whom he later formed a *liaison*. She was at that time the wife of an actor, K., though she looked like a young girl and, as she herself used to say, was in the habit of going, at the end of the opera or concert, to the stage door with the other girls to wave to "Herr Busch, who seemed all hearts to win". She was the most enchanting woman one could imagine, not so much because she was beautiful as

[1] National Sozialistische Deutsche Arbeiter Partei.

196

because she was kind, affectionate and full of childlike gaiety. Our little daughter called her "Frau Sonne";[1] a more appropriate name could not have been found. No one could understand why she had married K., a funny little man of improbable ugliness who specially distinguished himself as Wall in Shakespeare's *Midsummer Night's Dream*. She probably did it because she couldn't say "No" and—at any rate then—could not bear to vex anyone.

Later, when she had parted from K., Emmy made close friends with a man who was like a brother to us, a very cultivated person, who was thought highly of by our circle of friends. Through him she came to our house. Her magic was not merely external. It was much more her heart and character, her unembarrassed sincerity and transparent lack of affectation that made her irresistible. We took her to us with open arms.

After Emmy had got an engagement in Weimar she often came to Dresden. However gladly she would have come as a guest artist, she did not dare to take steps seriously in the matter because she was afraid of two professional colleagues who were known for their intrigues. "Fighting doesn't suit me," she said, and she was right. The most brilliant part that a woman could play in the Third Reich was to fall to her share in a different way.

During a symphony concert in the Opera House my wife was suddenly seized from behind and her eyes covered by a pair of gentle, perfumed hands. Emmy Sonnemann had arrived unexpectedly. When we asked if she would spend the evening with us she announced gaily, but with some embarrassment unusual with her, "You know—I've got a *chap* with me." It was Hermann Göring.

This free and easy description was not unsuitable to the heavy soldier in civilian clothes, who was presented to my wife and frightened her by the strength with which he shook hands.

It was impossible to picture Emmy's warmhearted and affectionate nature in connection with evil. Besides, she came of a respectable middle-class family, her background was domestic comfort and convention; she was the opposite of an adventuress

[1] Mrs. Sun.

197

or a light woman. Little by little we saw that she loved Göring sincerely and was resolved to attach her fate to his in lasting fashion. Her action seemed to guarantee the man.

In February 1933, towards the time when the battle against me in the Nazi press was reaching its highest point, Emmy Sonnemann telephoned suddenly to us, very late at night, to say, "Don't worry about those dreadful Dresdeners! I'm going to Berlin shortly to the State Theatre. Hermann wants nothing better than to get Fritz there too. Just think how nice it'll be there, all together!"

To the observation that I had a contract in Dresden she called back, laughing: "Oh, what does a contract mean! That's all nonsense!" and rang off.

I did not suspect that this night call would, a few weeks later, become of importance to me.

More dangerous than the Nazis' attempts to "liquidate" my salary—a measure existing only on paper so long as the constitution still held—was the reduction, actually carried out, of the opera budget by a third. It forced us to an economy which led in the first place to the dismissal of some of the younger members. A pretty *Sudeten* German girl begged me with tears to rescind the order, which I was not in a position to do. A few days later I found her announced as taking part in a National Socialist educational evening[1] and referred to as a Party member.

Shortly afterwards a detailed document, addressed to the head of the government, was laid before me in my office. It had a swastika on it and came from a Gauleiter, Cuno Meyer. According to this document, Fräulein Hildegard Tausche, one of the dismissed members, was a talented singer, such as the Dresden State Opera in its best days had hardly ever possessed, and the lack of appreciation for her could only be attributed to the pernicious attitude of the Musikdirektor. Cuno Meyer demanded, in the name of the Party, that the notice of dismissal should immediately be withdrawn; otherwise he would find himself obliged to take further steps against the Opera.

[1] Kulturabend.

198

I considered it was my business to answer Meyer. To my great annoyance, Reucker and the government official, Reuther, prevented my letter from being sent, in the mistaken belief that Reuther could still save the situation by prudence. I saw that it had already been lost.

My letter ran:

"Sir,

"On page 98 of the book *Mein Kampf* by Adolf Hitler I find the following lines: 'But this system (the Parliamentary system) by forcing the individual to pass judgment on questions for which he is not competent gradually debases his moral character. No one will have the courage to say, "Gentlemen, I am afraid we know nothing about what we are talking of. I least of all, in any case." '

"I am informed that you, Herr Meyer, are a manufacturer of artificial manure, while I have been professionally concerned with opera for twenty years. Acting in the spirit of the Führer I therefore suggest that you should deal with the case of Tausche by concerning yourself with your own dung heap and leaving me to the responsibility of mine.

"Your obedient servant,
"FRITZ BUSCH,
"Generalmusikdirektor of Saxony."

I caused the answer that I had wished to send to Gauleiter Meyer to be known as widely as possible so, as a member of the Rotary Club, I repeated it there and also spread it about in the theatre itself. The Nazis had their cells in both places; I have no doubt that the Party member, Meyer, even if my letter did not reach him, had full knowledge of its contents.

Some time in January 1933 the head of the Saxon Government, Schieck, summoned me to visit him. I valued him because he was unprejudiced and humane, and on account of the understanding that he brought to our Opera problems. I was less in agreement with what I considered a too great weakness in the conduct of the home politics of Saxony in face of the ever-growing insolence of the Nazis. As so often happened, there was here a case of a liberal *laisser faire* turning into weakness and encouraging the ruthless and unrestrained opponent to ever more daring demands.

Schieck felt it was his duty to draw my attention to the results of my attitude as an opponent of the Nazis. He was quite sure that in a few weeks there would be a complete political change and the government of Germany would fall into the hands of the National Socialists. My Intendant and I must then expect to be immediately dismissed from our posts. The Intendant—as he already knew—was to be replaced by an actor called Posse.

He went on with these words: "I am afraid that you, dear sir, will be sewn in a sack and thrown into the Elbe unless you decide at the last moment to change your behaviour completely and make concessions."

I told him that I quite agreed with his prediction, and he did not contradict me when I pointed out that he himself, though only a discreet antagonist of the system, ran the risk of sharing my fate. But I assured him that I should take care that two S.A. men, one on the left and one on the right, should go swimming arm-in-arm with me.

At the end of February I went to Copenhagen for a guest performance. On the sixth of March, the day after the elections for the Reichstag, I arrived back at midday in Berlin and before the train left for Dresden I had a conversation with my brother-in-law at the Anhalter Station. I told him of an extraordinary dream I had had a week before in Copenhagen. Not otherwise superstitious, I told it to both him and Rudolf Serkin, who was much alarmed by it. In this dream I experienced quite clearly the dramatic events which I was to encounter in the next few days. My brother-in-law, who was the solicitor entrusted with my affairs and a good friend of mine, listened to me and shook his head. Acquainted with the tense situation in Dresden, he urgently advised me, whatever happened, to do nothing rash.

A heavy, stout S.A. officer in a dazzling new uniform entered the dining-car ahead of me. When I asked my brother-in-law who really paid for all this luxury I was answered, "You."

I sat down beside Otto Klemperer, who was going to Budapesth for a guest performance. We had been friendly colleagues for years and I thought highly of him. Anyone who knows Klemperer's impulsive nature will easily understand that he made no attempt to control his expressions or the loudness of his voice. Nor am I one of those who, when they are excited, speak softly. The S.A. officer sitting next us could not have missed a single word of our talk, which was not charged with sympathy for the Nazi movement, Hitler's success or Germany's future under the new *régime*.

When we got out at Dresden I realised that the stout S.A. officer was Manfred von Killinger, who a few days later became the temporary successor of the head of the government, Schieck, and as such was to take the first measures against me. I had no right to blame him for the standpoint he took up.

On Tuesday the seventh of March I found myself in the office of the Generalintendant in the Taschenberg Palace. One felt the uncanny quietness before the storm, the thundery atmosphere which in the course of the day became ever more noticeable. It appeared inexplicable that they made difficulties when my wife wanted to exchange our official seats in the Opera House that night for tickets admitting to the Playhouse, though this had been customary for eleven years. Over and over again the box-office official tried to make sure whether on this evening she had really decided *not* to go to the opera. The reason for this we were still to learn.

In the afternoon, towards five o'clock, I went to the Opera House to prepare for the evening performance of *Rigoletto*. While I was reading the score, disturbances in the street and in the Opera Square became noticeable. It was said that swastika flags had been hoisted on the Opera House.

I was determined not to allow myself to be disturbed in my artistic concentration by any outward events.

To correct the inaccuracies in the music which are inevitable the daily repertory, I was in the habit of collecting all the singers in my room before the beginning of every performance.

Shortly before seven, a lady friend of the family who wished to come to the performance was announced. She entreated me with tears to leave the House at once, as she had heard the rumour that they intended "to kill the man Busch".

As always, at seven o'clock I began to rehearse the *ensembles* with the decidedly nervous singers. Suddenly the door opened. A heavily armed S.A. man entered. "Please, Herr General-musikdirektor, will you allow the singers to leave for a moment to take part in a *solemn affair*."

"Reluctantly," I said. "I need the rehearsal badly. Send the ladies and gentlemen back as soon as possible." I looked out of the window at the façade of the picture gallery opposite until, after about ten minutes, my singers returned.

Shortly afterwards a second S.A. man came in, a gigantic fellow, and requested me, this time in a much less friendly manner, to follow him on to the stage. In the middle of it, on a small platform, his back to the auditorium, stood the actor, Alexis Posse, an inferior man with a swollen head, and a bad comedian, who on the stage acted in small parts and in the Party an important role. Near him was his friend Schröder, just as insignificant. In a half-circle in front of them stood fifty to sixty S.A. men, impeccably dressed and fully armed. In the wings, some members of the orchestra, firemen, cloak-room attendants and scene-shifters had collected, as they usually do an hour before the beginning of a performance.

To this improvised audience Posse spoke of Hitler's taking over power, of the golden days which would dawn for art and the well-being of every individual, and also of how *I* was not suitable to achieve such aims and must consider myself removed from my post. As my successor he named the Kapellmeister Kutzschbach, and as a substitute Kapellmeister Striegler. With a "*Sieg Heil*" at which every arm except mine flew up in the air, the "solemn affair" concluded. Some malicious glances fell on me who, in my dress coat and my hands behind my back, stood on one side and did not move until the stage was clear.

Posse requested me, politely and explicitly, to conduct the performance. The singers therefore had to go back a third time to my room, to be released after a short, renewed rehearsal, for the performance.

Meanwhile, the Intendant and Government official had come in and heard what had happened to me. I placed myself at the conductor's desk. The audience—as was, of course, known to Posse—consisted almost exclusively of S.A. men and members of the Party. As it turned out later, the NSDAP had that morning given tickets for this performance to their fellow-members in the Dresden schools.

Hardly was my appearance observed when a wild outcry arose: "Down with Busch! Traitor, get out!" while I stood at my desk with my baton raised. The members of the Saxon State Orchestra who, eleven years before, had unanimously elected me as their conductor, sat in their seats pale and silent. The uproar grew, the noise increased; behind my back I heard the sounds of battle. Individual private persons who intimated they were in my favour with the cry, "Hoch, Busch!" came to blows with S.A. men. A member of the Teachers' Choral Society which I had often conducted, a man who had always shown a loyal attachment to me, was seized by the S.A., who threatened to throw him down from one of the balconies.

I did not turn round. As the roaring continued and the disturbance would not die down, after a few minutes I left the orchestra pit. I went into the Intendant's box, in which the Intendant and government official had witnessed the occurrence.

Kapellmeister Striegler was called for to take over the performance. "By accident" he happened to be in the House, a fact that seemed the more remarkable since as a rule in normal times he was more often searched for than found there.

After some hesitation, which he thought he ought to show for the sake of propriety, he went into the orchestra pit and I heard him received with applause and the beginning of the Prelude very inaccurately played by the orchestra.

At the moment at which I was preparing to go home, the attendant in charge of the boxes came up and with a very serious face begged me to use the side door to the Hotel Bellevue. At the chief entrance, which I generally used, S.A. men were standing who would fall upon me when I came out. I received with thanks the offer of the faithful Intendant to accompany me but I felt obliged to refuse it. Nor did I see why I should slink out by an emergency exit but felt entitled to use the route I had taken for eleven years.

At the exit, no one was there to strike me dead. I went home, where my youngest little daughter was just going to bed. She burst into tears when she suddenly saw her father, who should have been in the Opera House at this time, standing before her. But it was enough for her that I had not, as she expressed it, "got a knock".

My wife, who was intended to sit among the Nazis in the dress circle, and would have been a defenceless witness of the way I was treated, went to the Playhouse that evening with our son. A town councillor we knew went to her at once at the beginning of the performance and whispered that "something had happened" in the Opera House. My wife and son rushed home, where I had preceded them by a few minutes.

Friends who had been present at the incident in the Opera drank a glass of champagne with us. We were in the habit of meeting unusual events, whether cheerful or sad, in this way. While we were sitting together, the correspondent of a big American news agency rang up. I gave him a concise account of what had happened and its cause. My information was immediately communicated to the German and international press. At home there still reigned at the beginning of March 1933 a certain amount of freedom of the Press, so that the occurrences in the Dresden State Opera could be commented on in a friendly or inimical fashion according to the political attitude or personal courage of those responsible. The *Deutsche Allgemeine Zeitung* acted courageously with the headline: "Mediocrity makes itself important."

In the course of the night I dictated to my son a few pages of typewriting in which I defended myself against the calumnies that had sprung up. These pages on the one hand left no doubt as to my love for Germany, on the other hand showed that I stood on my rights of free participation in my own philosophy of life. This communication was sent next day to friend and foe alike.

As always when a well-known personage is overthrown, so in my case innumerable anonymous insulting letters were not lacking; but there were also many proofs of honourable disapproval of what had happened and manifestations of friendly feelings. And offers of leading positions soon followed.

On Wednesday, the eighth of March, there was a telephone call from my Intendant. The sixty-five-year-old man, speaking from a booth in the town in a voice he could hardly control from emotion, informed me that he had been dismissed from his post. Though formally refusing to accept this, he had to yield to force and was expelled from the Taschenberg Palace, which had been taken over by the S.A.

Posse, with the assistance of his colleague Schröder, now ruled in his place, while the business of the government official Reuther was taken over by the theatre hairdresser, Heger, and the swindler Börner had another administrative post. There was no longer any doubt that the fate of the Dresden Opera and the future of Art in the third Reich were now in the best hands.

On Thursday I was summoned to an interview with Posse in the Taschenberg Palace. The "temporary Intendant" began by inviting me to resume my work of conducting. I wished to know what had been brought forward against me. According to Posse it was (in this order):

1. Too many dealings with Jews.
2. Advantageous conditions offered to Jewish and foreign singers.
3. Too frequent absence.
4. A too high salary.

I refused to go into the old story of money and leave of absence, but referred Posse to my answer in writing in which I had proved how unfounded these allegations were in the only conclusive way, namely, by figures.

I protested that in engaging artists, no question of nationality or "race" should be raised. I declared clearly and cheerfully that I retained the right to choose my friends at my own discretion and did not intend to abandon them in their need. I refused to conduct any more.

It was evident to me that I had burnt my boats. No power in the world would have made me raise my baton again here. Even a telegram from Hitler to the Saxon Government ordering me to be immediately reinstated made no difference.

In my rapid career I had had to guard against people's importunities, the flattery and toadying which they always force on those who are the favourites of the public, but in spite of many professional battles and skirmishes there had never been a serious attack against my person. Now, at a single blow, the opposite was the case. Nasty looks, hatred extending even to the children at school and our devoted servants, who were actually threatened with physical violence—all this made me realise every day that, forced as I was into unwilling inaction, I was a fellow without a country, a depraved villain. Even the voices of those who, in the system of violence which was already clearly outlined, had had the courage to take my side were extinguished in the enormous garbage heap.

The Nazis' attack had been no surprise to me. As for a long time it had given me secret pleasure to defy the enemy, I had to be prepared for him to hit back. What enraged me was the *way* he had managed it. An insidious onslaught, as apparently spontaneous in effect as in reality carefully prepared, had been directed against the place where I worked, with the object of giving me my death blow there, before all the world. *That* triumph I grudged to the rabble.

I wanted my rights, that was all. That it was absurd to look for them from the Nazis is easy to see after the event. In the first days of the revolution I believed, like millions of others, that Germany was and would remain a law-abiding country.

At this moment I remembered Göring who, weeks before, had wished me to come to Berlin. It seemed that a better way of gaining justice could not be imagined. On Saturday the eleventh of March I left Dresden and went to Berlin.

I arrived exactly at the right moment to hear of Carl Ebert's dismissal from his position. While we were sitting at table in the Kempinski Restaurant, Ebert was informed that the Charlottenburg Opera House had been seized by the S.A. He at once hurried away there, was not admitted, and learnt next day that he had been dismissed.

Emmy Sonnemann arranged that I should meet Göring. I went to his private house. A Captain Körner took me into a spacious room hung with Gobelin tapestry; in the corner stood a big flag with a swastika on it. For the rest, the furniture seemed to be improvised, almost primitive, and had none of the later well-known luxury.

I had to wait a long time and, looking out of the window on to the street, saw the trucks with prisoners escorted by police or S.A. going past. When I turned round my glance fell on an open side door and I saw a big canvas on an easel, at which a painter was working. On a small platform sat Göring posing in a blue tunic, so that he might be handed down to posterity in oils. I wondered that he had time and nerves for such idle pleasures while in front of the windows of his house tragedies were being enacted.

The great man stepped quickly into the room, gave me his hand, and apologised for having kept me waiting. But he had no time now for a conversation as he "had to go to a ceremony of dedicating the flags".

The events at Dresden he described briefly as "filthiness"[1] which Hitler and he severely condemned, and "without more ado would have put right". He proposed to meet me in the afternoon in the Ministry of Home Affairs for a further discussion.

[1] Schweinerei.

207

I found Göring there in a spacious apartment, the back wall of which was again decorated by a huge black swastika on red cloth. From this first interview with him I got the impression of a man quick in the uptake who, as John Gunther truly remarked, was "capable of listening to what was said" and had enough breadth of mind to be able to understand the natural excitement and violent expressions of his interlocutor.

Our conversation lasted for more than an hour. After a few flattering remarks about me as a conductor, he declared, quickly and without ceremony or going into details, that the accusations raised against me were ridiculous. (He had been thoroughly informed beforehand as to my case, so I was later informed by one of the initiated.) He candidly blamed a set of Party men who had taken part in the affair, with expressions not generally used in polite German society, such as "filthy fellows", "little nincompoops" and similar terms. I replied that we were completely agreed about these gentry and added a few more epithets. My expressions became more and more violent, so that finally Göring interrupted me.

"You keep on abusing the Nazis," he said. "You ought at least to recognise that the Führer personally sent a telegram to Dresden, ordering them to reinstate you."

"That was no pleasure to me," I answered hotly.

I afterwards learnt that Hitler had sent a second telegram to Dresden to prevent any violence against me. He must have known his Pappenheimers.[1]

I told Göring most decidedly that at no price would I return to work at Dresden. He made an angry contemptuous gesture.

"That's not the question. Just wait a fortnight till I am president of the Cabinet. You know quite well that we should like to have you here."

I said I would not turn any Jewish colleague out of his

[1] In *Wallenstein's Tod* (Schiller) Wallenstein interviews Max Piccolomini, the leader of a famous regiment called the Pappenheimer. This is almost the last regiment to remain faithful to Wallenstein, who refers several times to "knowing his Pappenheimers".

position, and used the expression, "I can't collaborate in that."

Göring spoke of legal dismissals and monetary compensation. As I was still obstinate he became more vehement: "Well, my dear friend, you know we have means at hand to compel you!"

"Just try it, Herr Minister," I burst out. "A compulsory performance of *Tannhäuser* conducted by me would be no pleasure to you. You have never in your life heard anything that would be so stinkingly boring."

The strong expression only resulted in a cynically amused smile from Göring.

I went on to speak urgently of the only thing I had at heart—rehabilitation. After letting the injury to my reputation and the dirty Dresden agitation run their course for two months without paying any attention to them, the events of these last days were the last drops, and the cup had overflowed. They had roused my extreme indignation.

"I think," I ended excitedly, "you are making out my case too simple. Compared with me, Michael Kohlhaas[1] has a conciliatory nature."

Göring adopted a soothing manner.

"Well, don't excite yourself any more. I promise you that your affairs shall be put right. Meanwhile, just take a holiday for a fortnight."

At the door I turned round once more and begged him again, urgently, to prevent any call back to Dresden.

The people there were malignantly working for the same thing.

The triumvirate of hairdresser, comedian and swindler that now controlled the Dresden State Theatres had been joined by a Geheimrat Dr. A. as their new Generalintendant. Posse and Börner were subordinate, unintelligent men. (The former came to a miserable end on the St. Bartholomew's Night of the thirtieth of June 1934, while the latter, on account of forgery and other frauds, found himself in a concentration camp.) But

---

[1] A story by Heinrich von Kleist of a man who goes to abnormal lengths in fighting against an act of blatant injustice.

I considered the Geheimrat a dangerous creature. I could not bear him, nor he me.

The new Intendant was haunted by the idea of my return and had no peace. Others who bore a grudge against me for neglecting or offending them joined the worried man. A paper was placed for signing in the Opera House stating, among other things: "The undersigned request the Führer to take every means of preventing the former Musikdirektor Fritz Busch from returning to the Dresden Opera in any capacity whatever, as in personal and artistic matters he is incompetent."

A year previously, when a contract was known to have been offered to me to go to Berlin, the singers "filled with terror" had got their representative to write to me: "I implore you to stay! Stay with us!" Now, of over forty singers, seven had the courage to refuse their signatures.

A short time afterwards, Richard Strauss came to Berlin and we had a conference with Tietjen, the Intendant of the Prussian State Theatres, to discuss the affair of *Arabella*. Tietjen was watching over the interests of his absent colleague and friend, Reucker. Strauss declared it was to be taken for granted that the *première* of this work, dedicated to us both, would only be allowed if produced by Reucker and conducted by me. My remark that he was not to take me into consideration he put aside with decision. If I positively refused to conduct in Dresden then it should be somewhere else. There was no question of any other solution, as far as he was concerned.

When Strauss said this there is no doubt he was quite sincere. Many years later common friends assured me that he really tried to keep his word and withdrew the work in due form. Nevertheless, in the end he had to give way to the claims of the contracts he had signed. I myself do not know what then took place.

Not long after the conference with Tietjen I learnt from the newspapers that "the *première* of the opera *Arabella* conducted by Clemens Krauss and produced by Josef Gielen would take place in Dresden on July 1st".

At significant turning-points in my life I have sometimes

met with timely coincidences. On thinking over my position I remembered I had been repeatedly asked to conduct in Buenos Aires. I considered informing them over there that I was now free, but rejected the idea. The day after I received the Dresden pronouncement I was rung up by my wife, who had gone there in some anxiety to see after the children and the house. When she arrived she found a cable from the Colon Theatre[1] wishing to engage me for the coming season beginning in July.

A feeling of happiness at the approach of freedom filled me: I felt like an entombed prisoner who sees in the distance the first glimmer of daylight. But I was still too much trapped by my *idée fixe* to give the importance it deserved to the South American invitation.

I was sufficiently ingenuous for the idea of a public rehabilitation to hover in my mind. But it soon became apparent that the policy of the third Reich did not admit of such a proceeding. A withdrawal, or contradiction of the lies that had been broadcast about me, was not to be thought of. Hitler would never expose the Party to outsiders. His disapproval of the events in Dresden was kept absolutely secret. I should have known that all transactions of Party-members were sacred.

Another thing, however, I could *not* know—that is that Göring's power was more restricted than he himself imagined.

He would have liked to see me in a conductor's position in Berlin. When I had hurried to him in unrestrained indignation at the insults I had received in Dresden, he made all sorts of promises which he could not keep. Arrangements for the reorganisation of musical affairs thought necessary after Hitler had become Reich-Chancellor had been decided long ago. Hitler, like Wotan, the god to whom he had vowed himself, was "now the slave of his own law".[2] Like him, he would destroy whatever Göring tried to protect, just as Wotan destroyed Sigmund under Brünnhilde's shield.

It was characteristic of Göring's careless self-reliance that

---

[1] The celebrated Opera House of Buenos Aires.
[2] den Vorträgen nun Knecht. ("Walküre" IInd Act.)

these facts, which with all his projects and promises were doubtless known to him, left him entirely undisturbed.

National Socialism drove many people to madness. I was among the first who suffered this fate when I looked for honour from those who had no honour. In these evil weeks I fought to reinstate my sullied reputation as an artist and a man, without realising the idiotic uselessness of my action. But in a short space of time I came to my senses again. This happened at the moment at which freedom of choice was given back to me.

There was still *one* place in Germany which counterbalanced Berlin and this place made me an offer. Tietjen brought the conversation round to Bayreuth.

Toscanini, one of those who fought in the van for the endangered ideal of freedom, had already clearly established his humane attitude by a telegram in defence of colleagues who had been dismissed. Tietjen, also the chief artistic manager of the Bayreuth Festival, thereupon called in question the Maestro's willingness to work there as formerly.

"I am convinced he will not come," said he. "Frau Winifred Wagner will forget the resentment they still cherish in Wahn-fried on account of your crying off in 1925. I promise you that. Then you will conduct there instead of Toscanini."

I felt as if I had been hit on the head, said something or other to Tietjen and went away.

The devil carried me to a high mountain and said, "All this will I give thee . . ." He held my rehabilitation in his hand; friend and foe would realise what I had been imagining to myself day and night. The hand held out to me everything I desired; and I knew that I should not take it.

Toscanini, the man whose refusal to go to Bayreuth had been expected, had had his own experiences with despotism. He would have nothing to do with it. My struggles and refusal had been as obvious as his; but the Nazis were confident that I should suddenly turn against my own convictions. They smiled at my rejection of National Socialism as at the fleeting rebellion of so many who were now making their peace with it—those who blew the soup when it was too hot and then began to eat it.

How had I arrived at my conclusions?

One evening, walking along in the Tiergarten as it was growing dark, my wife abruptly quoted from Verdi's *Falstaff*: "What is honour?"

She thus gave me the impetus that had been lacking to make me realise that one either has honour or one hasn't. No one can give it or take it away.

From that time forward events began to drive us further afield. We became familiar with the thought of leaving Germany and made our preparations.

Frau Sonnemann sent us tickets for *Der Schlageter* by that Hanns Johst who "reached for his revolver when he heard the word *culture*". We soon saw that as far as this work was concerned, he could leave his murderous weapon quietly in his pocket. There was here no question of culture.

Our seats in the State Theatre were in the box next to Göring's, who meantime had become President of the Cabinet. In the interval he came up to me in the foyer. With some embarrassment he said hurriedly: "I can't keep my word to you. Sorry."

I bowed and said nothing.

"It distresses me very much," he went on. "I can to-day carry through everything in Germany that I want to, with one exception. Against the Führer's will I can and I will do nothing." He ended dramatically: "He is the only person to whom, all my life long, I will be subordinate."

I answered maliciously that I quite understood. I, too, had a sense of subordination.

Göring, though obviously trying to end the conversation, began to make other proposals. I shook my head. In the midst the bell rang. Göring became violent and said in a dictatorial voice: "Come, come, do what I say."

"Thank you very much—no, *Herr Ministerpräsident*."

The auditorium was beginning to darken as we entered our adjacent boxes. My wife looked at me. We went out as the curtain rose for the second act.

CODA

*We do not wish to make human beings into
state puppets, but to humanise the state.*

PESTALOZZI

THE first among us to leave the country was our nineteen-
year-old son Hans, who was already in Florence for the
Maggio Fiorentino, where he had met Carl Ebert, whose appren-
tice in the art of production he was to be. Our daughters were
told that we had decided they were to go to school in England.
From there we had had moving proofs of understanding and
readiness to help, even in the first days when the Dresden
scandal was circulating in the world press. To the intense
excitement of the children we also told them that we ourselves
were going to South America. I had promised to go there after
we had succeeded, in spite of the lateness of the hour and the
fact that the artists for Bayreuth and Salzburg had already completed their contracts, in collecting an excellent *ensemble* of
singers. I was able to take with me Ebert, Engel and a highly
talented young Hungarian assistant who had been dismissed
from Dresden, Robert Kinsky. The youngest member of the
expedition was my boy, who was to continue his preliminary
studies as unpaid producer's assistant at the Colon Theatre.

In my imagination I rolled up my sleeves in the joyful anticipation of starting work again. We had made practically no
savings, on account of the secure position at Dresden, to which
a considerable pension was attached. Our only possessions
abroad were a few thousand Swiss marks with which the first
expenses could be paid.

I was anxious, considering the Dresden attack, as to whether
we should get our passports; but we did, without difficulty.
On every passport we could take two hundred Reichsmarks
with us. This made, for the whole family, a working capital

of a thousand marks with which to lay the foundations of a new life.

In the early hours of the morning I had a last short conversation with Göring, at his private house. A few weeks had made a great change in the man. From an energetic, unaffected fellow he seemed to have become an ill-humoured, irritable Nero type, from whom nothing good was to be expected. He drummed nervously on the table with his fingers, while he again began speechifying. I entrenched myself behind the demand for rehabilitation which had not materialised. Göring's face became thoughtful.

"Yes—but you know—the Führer cannot expose the Party."

He pulled out of his pocket a small note-book to which a red pencil was attached, and made an entry in it. Still morosely he concluded:

"Really it would be better if it were all done some other way. When you come back from South America you shall conduct a Philharmonic Concert which the Führer will attend. At the conclusion we will come on to the platform and shake you by the hand . . . hey? Just you wait and see what the effect will be! More than anything that could be put into print at the moment."

("You'll wait a long time for that!" I thought. I don't know whether anyone else in my place would have *said* it.)

It was a relief to go away. This time the situation had been unpleasant.

Official invitations to conduct in the third Reich reached me seven times in the following years. I refused them all.

In the first days of May I took my daughters to England. I have never seen Germany again.

After staying for a few days with English friends I travelled across Holland to Zürich. At first I stayed with the Reiffs, delightful old friends of ours, whose cordial hospitality has been shown for many years to innumerable artists. Thomas Mann called the house—14 Mythenstrasse—*The Hostel for Genius*.

I often spent the evening at the Hotel Dolder, where my

Dresden friend, Albert Sommer, had taken refuge. Three months had not passed since Richard Strauss and Gerhardt Hauptmann had been received and honoured in his cultivated home. Now it had been looted by Saxon members of the Party and its owner forbidden to return. Besides Dr. Sommer, I met at the Hotel Dolder the internationally known Berlin criminal lawyer Dr. Alsberg, a melancholy, broken man, who, a few weeks later, ended his own life.

In Zürich I received an invitation from Toscanini to a reception he was giving in his house on one of the Borromeo Islands which he had rented from an Italian aristocrat. Although my brothers proposed that I should make the journey with them and Serkin I at first refused. The experiences of the last months had depressed me too much. My wife, who was still in Germany occupied with winding up our affairs, wrote to me, however, advising me to accept, as she hoped it would distract me from the state of mind I was in. So I decided to go to Pallanza.

On the island, to my horror, I met several hundred people excitedly discussing the state of affairs; besides musicians there were writers, such as Emil Ludwig, Erich Maria Remarque and many others. In no mood to join the crowd, I hurried out into the spacious gardens. Suddenly I came up against Toscanini, who was doing the same. I thought he wished to be free from "the spirits he had summoned".[1] It was not so easy for him. Hardly had we exchanged a few words when a telegram was brought to him. He took it with a sigh and held it close to his weak eyes in the attempt to decipher it.

"*Scusi*," he said. "It is for you, from the Signora."

I read it and explained to the Maestro, who was full of curiosity, that my wife knew how unwilling I had been to go to a big reception. "So she has just telegraphed only three words—*Coraggio, tesor mio*."

This is the beginning of an Italian soldiers' song, which Toscanini of course knew, and we laughed.

[1] Die ich rief, die Geister,
Werd ich nun nicht los. Goethe. *Der Zauberlehrling.*

"Do stay here to-night after the guests have gone," said Toscanini. "I want very much to speak to you."

I felt that he was much preoccupied. When, later, we were alone in his room, he showed me a letter from Hitler, in which he declared how happy he would be "to welcome the great Maestro of the friendly Italian nation to Bayreuth before long". A few years before, a Fascist horde had fallen upon the elderly Maestro with physical violence. Something similar, perhaps even worse, had happened to me. Both he and I had come to recognise that the appearance of wounded honour means nothing compared to the true shame of serving wickedness.

What was depressing Toscanini, from his youth closely attached to the art of Richard Wagner, and its greatest interpreter, was anxiety for the future of the Bayreuth Festival. Feeling thus he asked me, "What will Bayreuth do if I refuse?"

"Then they will invite me, Maestro," I said.

Toscanini was speechless.

"That is to say, they *have* invited me. Tietjen, who expects your refusal, has already taken steps."

I was delighted at his astonishment and added with a laugh, "Of course, I will refuse, like you."

Toscanini shut his mouth, which had remained open from astonishment, and purred, in his warm, melancholy voice, "*Eh, caro amico!*"

We were both silent, and a feeling of great sorrow came over us.

A few days later my wife arrived in Bâle and I told her of my conversation with Toscanini. For the last time we went for a walk in the neighbourhood and looked out at Germany— our country lay before our eyes. If Toscanini had meanwhile made his refusal the summons to me might come at any moment. We went across to Zürich to the Dolder Hotel and visited our friends. After dinner I was sent for to take a long-distance call from Berlin. Tietjen was at the telephone.

"Toscanini has just refused Bayreuth. Will you conduct? I invite you in the name of Frau Winifred Wagner."

"Give my best thanks to Frau Wagner. I thank you, too, dear Herr Tietjen. But in two weeks I am sailing for Buenos Aires. You will certainly understand that one must keep one's word."

Tietjen understood me perfectly.

In the course of the evening I met my old friend Bronislaw Hubermann, a *Pan-European*, as I was. We spoke of what had happened, and marvelled at the skill of the Gestapo, which had been able to find me directly, in the Dolder Hotel, where I was only staying on a visit, without going round about or making further inquiries. I have established the fact that a call to ask for me at the Reiffs' house never followed.

At that moment I was called to the telephone again. This time it was my brother Adolf. Toscanini had asked him what Fritz had done when he—Toscanini—had refused Bayreuth.

I promised to inform the Maestro immediately. While we were considering the Italian text my wife had a brain-wave. "Let us simply telegraph the end of the song, "*Coraggio, tesor mio!*" So we wired, adding "*Ho rifiuto anch' io*"[1] to Maestro Toscanini, Pallanza.

"L'armata se ne va,
Se non partiss' anch' io,
Sarebbe una viltà!"[2]

Richard Strauss sprang into the breach at Bayreuth. In Milan we met the Eberts. Erich Engel and his wife were to join us at Villefranche. Our son came from Rome. Only my wife had to remain in uncertainty. If all went well she was to follow with our two daughters.

On the 15th of June 1933 the *Conte Biancamano* left the harbour of Genoa to take us to a new, free world.

[1] I have refused as well.
[2] The army is leaving. If I did not go too it would be an act of cowardice.

INDEX